FRANKLIN DELANO ROOSEVELT

FOR *Kids*

His Life and Times with 21 Activities

Richard Panchyk

CHICAGO REVIEW PRESS

**Library of Congress
Cataloging-in-Publication Data**

Panchyk, Richard.
  Franklin Delano Roosevelt for kids : his
life and times with 21 activities / Richard
Panchyk. — 1st ed.
      p. cm.
  Includes bibliographical references and
index.
  ISBN-13: 978-1-55652-657-2
  ISBN-10: 1-55652-657-1
  1. Roosevelt, Franklin D. (Franklin
Delano), 1882–1945—Juvenile literature.
2. Presidents—United States—Biography—
Juvenile literature. 3. Roosevelt family—
Juvenile literature. 4. United States—Politics
and government—1933-1945—Juvenile
literature. 5. Creative activities and seat
work—Juvenile literature. I. Title.
  E807.P26 2007
  973.917092—dc22
  [B]
                                   2007003484

"Decode a Navy Signal Flag Message" activity, page 31, was adapted with permission from *Sailors, Whalers, Fantastic Sea Voyages* by Valerie Petrillo.

Excerpt on page 79 from *A Lifelong Affair: My Passion for People and Politics* ©Bethine Church (Francis Press), reprinted with permission of the author.

Cover and interior design: Monica Baziuk

Cover images ★ Courtesy Library of Congress: Eleanor Roosevelt, "Little White House," migrant family ★ Courtesy Franklin D. Roosevelt Presidential Library and Museum: FDR with Fala and girl, young Franklin on pony, soldiers at Normandy, FDR in car ★ Courtesy National Archives: soldiers at Iwo Jima, girl conserving tin ★ All other images courtesy of the author.

Interior images ★ Courtesy Library of Congress: page 6 (right): LOC HABS NY, 14-HYP, 5-3; page 25: LOC LC-USZ62-10466; page 35: LOC LC-USZ62-113659; page 58: LC-USF34-009093-C; page 61: LOC LC-USA7-18241 DLC; page 62: LOC LC-USZ62-18168 DLC; page 65: LOC LC-USZ62-26759 (top), LC-USZ62-108091 (bottom); page 71: LC-USZC2-5733 (left), LC-USZC2-1162 (right); page 75: LOC LC-USZ62-11491; page 96: LOC LC-USZ62-5436 DLC; page 98: LOC LC-USZ62-15185; page 114: LOC-USZ62-25600; page 122: LOC LC-USZ62-7449; page 124: LOC LC-USZ62-104519; page 128: LOC LC-USZ62-88060 DLC; page 129: LOC LC-USZ62-67439 ★ Courtesy Franklin D. Roosevelt Presidential Library and Museum: pages 6 (left), 9, 10, 11, 13, 15, 18, 19, 26, 29, 33, 43, 44, 47, 49, 55, 67, 72, 88, 101, 108, 110, 112, 118, 119, 121, 134 ★ Courtesy National Archives: pages ix, 7, 64, 107 ★ page 87: courtesy Vera Fairbanks ★ page 132: photo by William B. Harvay ★ Page 140: http://en.wikipedia.org/wiki/Franklin_D._Roosevelt_Memorial ★ All other images courtesy of the author.

Published by Chicago Review Press, Incorporated
814 North Franklin Street
Chicago, Illinois 60610
ISBN-13: 978-1-55652-657-2
ISBN-10: 1-55652-657-1
Printed in China

5   4   3   2   1

For Matt and Beth

CONTENTS

TIME LINE

1640s The first Roosevelts arrive in the New World

1828 James Roosevelt (Franklin Roosevelt's father) born

1856 Sara Delano (Franklin Roosevelt's mother) born

1882 Franklin Delano Roosevelt born

1884 Anna Eleanor Roosevelt born

1898 Spanish-American War begins

1900 James Roosevelt dies

1901 President William McKinley assassinated; Vice President Theodore Roosevelt becomes president

1905 Franklin and Eleanor Roosevelt are married

1906 Franklin and Eleanor's first child, Anna Eleanor, born

1910 Franklin Roosevelt elected to the New York State senate

1912 Franklin Roosevelt named assistant secretary of the navy in Woodrow Wilson's administration

1914 World War I begins

FOREWORD

by Tobie Roosevelt (Mrs. Franklin D. Roosevelt Jr.)

How could I have ever imagined, as I was growing up, that one day I would carry one of the most recognizable names in the world? Before we married, I was asked by my future husband, the son and namesake of the president, if I was sure I wanted to have his name. I couldn't imagine what he meant. He explained that for his whole life this mantle had been a weight on his shoulders, and my life would never be the same once I became Mrs. Franklin D. Roosevelt Jr. Wherever FDR Jr. traveled around the world, people were drawn to him. He even looked like his father. He would walk into a room and command attention.

Though I never had the privilege of meeting the president, my husband spoke very lovingly about his father. He remembered what fun he had growing up at "Springwood," the house in Hyde Park, and spending summers on Campobello Island with his parents and grandmother. One of FDR Jr.'s most cherished memories was of sailing with his father. In spite of his physical handicap, FDR continued to sail and passed on his love of the sea to Franklin Jr. My husband had a very strong bond of love and respect with his father.

President Roosevelt left an immense legacy. In this book you will read the story of FDR's life, including his perseverance in learning to live with polio. This fight gave him strength and a spirit that he took with him when he was elected president. He brought our country through difficult times at home and abroad. He preserved freedom for us to grow and flourish as a nation. FDR showed the ability to overcome that which seemed impossible at the time. Strength, optimism, vitality, and stamina were all characteristics of FDR's life. As you grow into adulthood, try to incorporate these four characteristics into your life. Take advantage of and learn from FDR's legacy—set your sights high and go for your goals.

FOREWORD

by Senator Edward M. Kennedy

FRANKLIN ROOSEVELT WAS elected president the year I was born. He was a leading topic of conversation in our family and across the nation for the next 13 years. My father knew him well and was a friend of President Roosevelt. He named my father the first chairman of the Securities and Exchange Commission and later appointed him ambassador to Great Britain.

My three older brothers, Joe, Jack, and Bobby, talked about President Roosevelt with my father, and, listening to those conversations, I thought that he must be a good person and a good leader for our country, and for the world. I knew he was a Democrat!

When I was six, my parents took me with them to London because President Roosevelt had asked my father to become America's ambassador to Great Britain. I knew it was an important assignment, but I was totally surprised by the British people. They seemed to treat us almost like royalty, and wherever we went, they wanted to take our pictures. I was amazed to see my photo in the newspaper too. Unfortunately, only a year later, war broke out in Europe. My father stayed on, but it was so dangerous that my mother brought me home. But my father's service to FDR stayed in my mind. I was proud of him, and that experience certainly influenced my later decision to go into public service myself. I also had immense respect for President Roosevelt, and all he did for our country. The New Deal always meant something special to me ever since.

A letter from young Bobby Kennedy to FDR, 1935.

Author's Note

$\mathcal{F}$ RANKLIN DELANO ROOSEVELT often went by his initials, FDR, throughout his life. In fact, he was still a child when he began signing his letters "FDR." Later, when he was president, it was a way to distinguish him from former president Theodore Roosevelt. When discussing Roosevelt in the first two chapters of this book, while he is still a young man, I refer to him mostly as Franklin. Later, when he enters politics and marries, I use FDR, Franklin, and Roosevelt alternately. Regardless of the nickname used, I am always referring to Franklin Delano Roosevelt.

I have included first-person narratives throughout the book, and I was fortunate to be able to speak to several people who knew FDR. The people whose stories appear on these pages include the son of Franklin D. Roosevelt's treasury secretary, the daughter of Vice President Henry Wallace, the son of President Dwight Eisenhower, and the grandson of President Woodrow Wilson. Their insight and stories are extremely valuable, and I let them speak to you, the readers, directly. I hope you will find it interesting to read firsthand what FDR's eldest grandchild, for example, remembers about her grandparents.

In researching this book, I used sources dating from 1932 to the present. This gave me perspective on the changing views of FDR over time. It reinforced for me the fact that history is remembered according to who is writing it, and when.

I hope that you will enjoy reading this book as much as I enjoyed writing it.

ACKNOWLEDGMENTS

T HE FIRST PERSON I should thank is Chris Breiseth at the Franklin and Eleanor Roosevelt Institute for his tremendous support and encouragement, and for putting me in touch with all the right people.

Sincere thanks also to Ellie Seagraves for her wonderful stories and insight. Thanks to Anna Eleanor Roosevelt for her encouragement. Very special thanks to the delightful Mrs. Franklin D. Roosevelt Jr. for her support of my project and for her foreword, and to the very kind Senator Edward M. Kennedy for his foreword.

Also thanks to all the other illustrious contributors, namely Jimmy Carter, Schuyler Chapin, Anne Cox Chambers, Bethine Church, Jean Wallace Douglas, Michael Dukakis, John SD Eisenhower, Vera Fairbanks, Geraldine Ferraro, Warren G. Harding III, Kitty Carlisle Hart, Clare Harvay, Adelaide Daniels Key, Theodore W. Kheel, the late Jeane Kirkpatrick, Matthys Levy, David Russell Luke, George McGovern, Robert Morgenthau, Peter Prommersberger, Kermit Roosevelt, Robert Rosenman, Reverend Francis B. Sayre Jr., Helen "Gig" Smith, and Victoria Wirth, for taking the time to make important contributions to this book.

Thanks as well to Helen Hannah Campbell, Forrest Church, and Margaret Truman Daniel for their correspondence and support. Thanks to Ingrid Molinazzi, Sara Williams, and James Kennedy for their persistence.

Thanks of course to my family, Caren, Matthew, and Elizabeth, for their support. And thanks to Cynthia Sherry and Lisa Reardon for believing in this important project.

THE ROOSEVELTS OF HYDE PARK

As Franklin Delano Roosevelt took the presidential oath of office on March 4, 1933, his hand rested on the Roosevelt family Bible. The Bible dated to 1686 and was written in Dutch. In that treasured Bible, Franklin Roosevelt's ancestors had written a record of the long Roosevelt lineage. FDR, as he was known throughout his life, was very proud of his ancestry. Though his ancestors were luminous, FDR's brightness would outshine them all.

The Roosevelt Ancestry

The Roosevelt story begins sometime during the late 1640s, when the New World was still very new to the Europeans. Claes Martenszen van Rosenfelt and his wife, Jannetje, left their home in Holland, stepped onto a ship, and set sail for the mysterious and alluring land of America. Though the English had settlements in Massachusetts and Virginia, among other places, the Dutch had their own foothold in the New World. A few weeks later, Claes and Jannetje set foot in the little Dutch settlement of New Amsterdam, located at the tip of Manhattan Island (the beginnings of what is now New York City). Their name, van Rosenfelt, was Dutch for "from the field of roses." Their coat of arms features three roses at the center.

The thriving town of New Amsterdam, founded only about 20 years earlier, was filled with a few hundred enterprising Dutch and English settlers who, like Claes and Jannetje, had come to America to seek their fortune. Claes and Jannetje soon adjusted to life in the New World. They had six children beginning in about 1650. Unfortunately, Claes died in 1659 and Jannetje soon after.

In 1664, a British fleet sailed into New Amsterdam harbor, and the governor, Peter Stuyvesant, surrendered without any shots being fired. From then on, both the city and the larger colony were to be known as New York. It was a peaceful transition, and the Dutch influence in New York remained strong for the next 100 years. Many of the early Dutch families became very wealthy and respected in social circles.

Though not very much else is known about the early lives of Claes and Jannetje's children, within a few generations, the Roosevelts were among the richest and most respected families in the state of New York.

Claes and Jannetje's son Nicholas Roosevelt (1658–1742) was the common ancestor of two future presidents and a future first lady. The branch of the family from which President Theodore Roosevelt was descended eventually moved to Oyster Bay, in Long Island, New York, and was founded by Johannes Roosevelt. His brother Jacobus (also known as James) was the ancestor of Franklin's branch of the family. Jacobus and Johannes invested money in Manhattan real estate.

Franklin Roosevelt's great-great-grandfather was a sugar merchant who became known as Isaac the Patriot (1726–1794) for his financial support of the American Revolution. He was later president of the first bank in New York and one of its first state senators.

After several generations living in New York City, in 1818, Isaac's son James (1760–1847) sold his land in Manhattan and moved the Roosevelt family about 70 miles north of the city on the east side of the Hudson River, to a house he called Mount Hope. James had a son named Isaac (1790–1863). Isaac was Franklin's grandfather, though he died long before Franklin was born. He attended medical school at Columbia University, but he never actually practiced medicine. Isaac moved back to Mount Hope until he married and had a child, then he moved a short distance away to a home he called Rosedale.

The child was Franklin D. Roosevelt's father, James Roosevelt (1828–1900). After attending the University of New York (in Manhattan) and then Union College in upstate New

York, James Roosevelt traveled for a year and a half in Europe when he was in his 20s, even briefly joining the fight for a free Italy in 1848. James was a wealthy lawyer and businessman who was involved in coal, railroad, and canal companies and investments. In 1872, he was elected president of the Southern Railway Security Company. James married Rebecca Brien

What's in a Name?

BY ANNA ELEANOR ROOSEVELT,
granddaughter of Franklin and Eleanor Roosevelt

"What's in a name? Apparently, my family felt a name carried some significance because they used the same names over and over again. My cousin Theodore is Theodore Roosevelt IV. Jameses and Annas and Eleanors and Saras—and their derivatives—abound. It's a nice tradition, but one that should come with a 'user's manual.'

Does being named for someone mean you have to be like them—as successful, as smart, as generous, as tragic? Names should come with stories, or at least with taglines! Something to go on, as you grow up and try to find your own self.

While no one is exactly like an ancestor, legacy is a powerful tool to help us discover our strengths, talents, and preferences. Knowing about who we might be named after can help us 'own up' to what, deep inside, we know about ourselves. How alike am I—or, how different? And why?

My grandmother would not want me to be just like her. But knowing about her shyness and how she handled it helped me to identify my own shyness and to think through why I felt that way and what to do about it.

Names have the power of the past. How can we know where we're going if we don't know who has gone before us?"

⇒ Chart Your Cousins

FRANKLIN'S PARENTS WERE sixth cousins. Franklin and Eleanor Roosevelt were fifth cousins. Many of the Roosevelts and Delanos married distant cousins. But what does it mean to be fifth cousins? How closely were they related? To be first cousins with someone means that you have the same grandparents. To be second cousins, you have the same great-grandparents, and so on. Fifth cousins have the same great-great-great-great-grandparents—ancestors about 200 years in the past. In Franklin and Eleanor Roosevelt's case, their common Roosevelt ancestor was Nicholas Roosevelt. Fifth cousins are far enough removed that people who have not done much genealogy could actually marry each other and be fifth cousins without ever knowing it. In this activity you will see what you can find out about your cousins.

YOU'LL NEED
* Paper
* Pen or pencil

Make a list of your first cousins. Do you have any first cousins once removed—children of first cousins? Now, can you identify second cousins? These are the grandchildren of your great-aunts and great-uncles. Can you go any further back than that? Next, make a chart of the first and middle names in your family, including parents, sisters and brothers, nieces and nephews, aunts and uncles, grandparents and their siblings, and any farther back you can go. Do you see names repeated from one generation to the next?

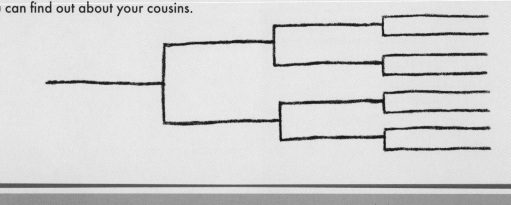

Howland (1831–1876) in 1853, and the couple had a son named James Roosevelt Roosevelt (nicknamed "Rosy") in 1854.

After a fire gutted Mount Hope in 1866, James Roosevelt and family moved further north, to an estate of several hundred acres at first called Springwood, and then known as Hyde Park (after the town in New York in which it was located). Rebecca Howland Roosevelt died of a heart attack in 1876. James remarried in October 1880, this time to his sixth cousin, the 26-year-old Sara Ann Delano (1854–1941), whom he'd met at a New York City dinner party held by one of his cousins. Sara was the same age as James's son from his first marriage, and was soon to become mother to James's second child, Franklin.

The Delano Ancestry

Sara Delano also came from a long and respected American lineage. Her great-great-great-great-grandfather Philippe de la Noye had arrived in the New World in 1621, not long after the original Pilgrims. Her grandfather Warren Delano and her great-grandfather Ephraim Delano were both sea captains. Sara's wealthy father, Warren Delano II, had built a successful career in the shipping business and spent many years in China and

Hong Kong building his fortune. Though James Roosevelt was wealthy, Warren Delano was about three times wealthier.

Though she was born in the United States, Sara Delano spent several years in Hong Kong as a child, before her family returned to the United States after the Civil War. The Delanos were a large family. There were 10 children in all, though four of them died before Franklin was born. The ancestral name de la Noye was not forgotten over the years; one of Sara Delano's brothers was named Philippe de la Noye Delano.

Sara and her siblings grew up on the 60-acre estate (known as Algonac) of her parents, on the west side of the Hudson River near Newburgh, New York, across the river from the Roosevelts. The Delanos were recent transplants from Massachusetts, having only arrived in New York State in 1852. Sara had several sisters—Laura, Annie, Kerrie, and Dora.

Sara Delano's sister, Annie Lyman Delano, in 1870. "Aunt Annie" was one of Franklin Roosevelt's favorite family members.

Franklin's Childhood

On the evening of January 30, 1882, Sara Delano Roosevelt gave birth to a son in an upstairs room in the Roosevelt mansion at Hyde Park. At 10 pounds, he was a big, healthy baby. Still, Sara and her newborn almost died because Sara had been given too much chloroform during the birth. He was named after his mother's uncle, Franklin Delano. By the time baby Franklin Delano Roosevelt was born, his half brother James was nearly 28 years old, so Franklin was essentially raised as an only child. James, nicknamed "Rosy," had by then married a member of the Astor family, one of the richest and most powerful dynasties in the country.

One of Franklin's first memories was from when he was three years old, on a ship with his parents, returning from Europe to New York. During the trip, a huge wave overcame the ship and nearly capsized it. A few men were washed overboard. Franklin had to wait in the upper berth of the cabin as water flooded in. Franklin stayed calm during the crisis. He only grew alarmed once he noticed that his toy jack had fallen into the water. The bad experience on the ship did not discourage his parents, who took Franklin to Europe regularly during his childhood.

As Franklin took his first steps, his devoted parents were there for him. As he grew, his mother enjoyed dressing him in adorable suits, which little Franklin did not care for so much. His mother let his hair grow long until she felt she needed to cut it, even though she would have preferred to keep it long. It was clear early on that young Franklin was a very intelligent child. He could be charming and talkative at times, but he also seemed perfectly content alone. He was confident and independent;

(right) The Roosevelts' Hyde Park, New York, estate. (below) Franklin Roosevelt at age four.

though he did not have many friends his own age, he was able to play well by himself. He liked to listen to the stories that his nurse, a woman he called Mamie, told him.

The first documented letter that Franklin ever wrote (at the age of five), was a note [punctuation added] he wrote to his mother hoping she was feeling better:

"Dear Sallie,

I am very sorry you have a cold and you are in bed. I played with Mary today for a little while. I hope by tomorrow you will be able to be up. I am glad today that my cold is better.

Your loving,
Franklin D. Roosevelt"

When Franklin was five years old, he traveled with his parents to Washington, D.C., where he got to meet President Grover Cleveland (his father knew the president, who was from New York State). The second-term president leaned over to young Franklin and told him, "My little man, I am making a strange wish for you. It is that you may never be president of the United States." Cleveland had gone through a particularly rough campaign against the Republican nominee James G.

Blaine in 1884, in which scandals and lies were gossiped.

As a boy, Franklin cultivated an interest in numerous hobbies. For one, young Franklin loved building model ships. He also enjoyed collecting toy soldiers and acting out battles with them. For Christmas one year, he asked for two boxes of soldiers with "two little cannons hitched to horses and 10 little soldiers with white trousers and blue jackets."

One of the pastimes Franklin enjoyed most was stamp collecting. He started this hobby when he was nine years old. He liked to lie on his stomach and examine and catalog his stamps. This childhood hobby was no passing fancy. Franklin continued to take great interest in stamps for the rest of his life.

Though Franklin was schooled at home, his lessons were not conducted haphazardly. He had regular hours of study from 9 A.M. to noon, and then again after lunch until 4 P.M. Though he rebelled against this orderly schedule once, he soon realized that it was better to have a routine than to be left completely to his own devices.

Franklin had a series of governesses and tutors who taught him, among other things, German and French. By the time he was seven, he was able to write a short note to his mother entirely in German, and at the age of 10 he wrote a letter to his parents entirely in

One of FDR's early drawings.

FRANKLIN ROOSEVELT probably did more for stamp collecting as a hobby than any other person in American history. By the 1890s, Franklin was an avid stamp collector. He spent hours at a time with his collection, using his magnifying glass to examine the condition and details of each stamp. Later, FDR took a great interest in stamps released during his presidency, approving all stamps and making suggestions for their design.

YOU'LL NEED

★ Scissors
★ Small, shallow bowl
★ Tweezers
★ Magnifying glass
★ Stamp-collecting price guide (such as *The Official Blackbook Price Guide of United States Postage Stamps*)
★ Stamp mounts (optional—available from a hobby store)

The first U.S. stamps were released in 1847 and featured Benjamin Franklin (5 cents) and George Washington (10 cents). By the late 1860s, designs included an eagle and shield, a locomotive, and Christopher Columbus landing in the Americas.

Collecting stamps is easy. Everyone has unused stamps around the house, and everyone receives mail with used (cancelled) stamps on it. While new stamps are more valuable, cancelled stamps are also highly collectable.

Start your collection by asking your parents for one of each design and denomination (value) of stamp in the house. Stamp mounts (small, black-backed plastic sleeves) are a good place to keep individual stamps, which can be slipped in without compromising the stamp adhesive. These can be mounted into a notebook or binder. In the old days, gummed hinges were applied directly to stamps to adhere them into books, but this could damage the stamps.

You can add to your collection with each day's mail. Ask for any envelopes that will be thrown away. Cut out the corner of the envelope with the stamp(s). Put about an inch of warm water into a bowl, and place the piece of envelope into it, with the stamp faced down. After five minutes, remove the paper from the bowl with tweezers. The stamp should peel off the paper easily. If it resists, get more warm water and give it another minute or two. Lay the wet stamp face down on a flat, water-resistant surface to dry. If it curls a bit, once dry you can place it under a heavy book to flatten it. The best used stamps are ones that have not been cancelled so heavily that the cancellation marks smear, or so lightly that they appear faint. The best unused stamps have all their gum intact (if they are gummed), have perfect perforations, and are centered well (some stamps are slightly off center).

Each stamp issued by the U.S. Postal Service has an official catalog number from Scott's (publisher of stamp books and catalogs). The number "1" was issued to the first stamp in 1847. The Scott's publications are helpful in cataloging your collection and determining the release dates of stamps. How many stamps can you collect and catalog in two weeks?

The envelope from a letter sent to FDR while he was president. He kept some of these for his stamp collection.

French. When he was nine years old, during one of the family's trips to Europe, Franklin spent several weeks attending school in Germany. Another time he took a side trip into Switzerland with his tutor.

Sports and the Great Outdoors

The sprawling country property his wealthy parents owned was a paradise to young Franklin. He was encouraged to explore the grand estate and enjoy the wonders of the outdoors. He was fascinated by the plants and animals that surrounded him, and he would spend hours on end outside.

With the Hudson River practically outside the Roosevelts' door, a love of the water was natural, and Franklin sometimes swam in the Hudson River or in a pond on the estate. In winter, Franklin enjoyed snowshoeing and ice skating. One of his favorite boyhood books was called *History of Sea Power*. His mother figured that some of his love for the sea and for ships was inherited from the Delano side of the family.

Animals were of special interest to Franklin. He enjoyed playing with his dog, a red setter named Marksman, and riding his pony, Debbie. He had been given his first dog at the age of five, and the pony followed at age seven. Franklin also took an early interest in birds, at first just watching and identifying them, and collecting specimens of their eggs. When he was only 11 years old, he got his own gun. His mother made him promise he would kill only one male and one female of each species, and nothing during nesting season.

Franklin set about to shoot specimens of each of the local birds in the Hudson River Valley. He even tried mounting his catch, but decided that gutting and stuffing the birds was not quite for him, and from then on he had them professionally stuffed. One by one, the trophy birds were added to the display cabinet that sat proudly in the family library. Some of the bird specimens he collected were oriole, heron, robin, hawk, and woodpecker. Before long, he had a complete collection of all the birds that were native to his Hudson River Valley area.

One of Franklin's favorite field trips was to the Museum of Natural History in New York City. There, he could gaze in awe at the many specimens of animals, the gems and minerals, and other natural wonders. Hearing of Franklin's enjoyment, his grandfather Delano bought him a lifetime membership to the museum. When he was 14, Franklin was delighted to get a chance to see birds in the South Kensington Museum in London.

FDR and his mother (above); FDR and his father (top), 1888.

➤ Go Bird-Watching

YOUNG FRANKLIN Roosevelt loved bird-watching and became an expert on the bird species native to New York. In this activity you will identify as many different bird species as you can and keep a record of each type of bird you see for two weeks.

YOU'LL NEED
- ★ Binoculars
- ★ Notebook
- ★ Field guide to North American birds or birds of your region (such as the Peterson series of guides)
- ★ Pen or pencil
- ★ Folding chair

Use your field guide to find out what bird species are native to your state and what migratory bird species stop in your area on their way somewhere else. Now gather your binoculars, notebook, pen or pencil, and folding chair, and head outdoors.

The best places to look for birds are where they make nests, where they look for food, and where they socialize. Trees, bushes, shrubs, bird feeders, birdbaths, open grassy areas, fences, and telephone and electric lines are all good places to look for birds. Bushes that yield berries, such as holly, are likely to attract birds. Note that birds are most plentiful when flowers and trees are in bloom. In some colder areas, many bird species fly south for the winter. In mild climates, birds may be spotted in all seasons. Once you find your spot for bird watching, set up a chair and observe. Find a vantage point that is at least 15 to 20 feet from a tree or bush. Try to be still, so as not to scare birds away.

There are several characteristics to note about a bird in order to identify it. What is its shape? Is it long and thin, or is it rounded? What colors or markings does it have (for example, does it have a spot on its neck, or a colored patch on its tail)? What is the shape of the tail? Is it forked, rounded, or square? If you use binoculars, you may be able to tell the shape and relative size of the beak. Make notes, and leaf through your field guide to try and identify the birds you see.

In your notebook, chart how many times you see a particular type of bird over the two weeks and when. You might want to vary the times you go out bird-watching to see if birds in your area are more active at certain times of day.

Fishing was another of his favorite activities. He enjoyed catching tiny minnows with his father. Franklin also took an active interest in trees. The huge property at Hyde Park had a great assortment of trees, and Franklin himself planted thousands of trees there over the years.

It seemed that Franklin was always building something. Once, he and a friend built a boat-shaped tree house to play in. Another time, he planned to build a yacht club with his friend.

In addition to the Hyde Park estate, the family owned a beautiful three-story summer cottage on Campobello Island, two miles off the coast of Maine, in the Bay of Fundy (part of the province of New Brunswick, Canada). It was there that the future president learned how to sail, first on his 21-foot boat, and then

FDR on a pony at age seven, in 1889.

on the 40-foot *Half-Moon* (named after the ship the explorer Henry Hudson sailed up the Hudson River in 1609). The wealthy Roosevelts also owned a townhouse in Manhattan, where they spent winters to avoid the cold and snowy Hyde Park area. Franklin also spent time with members of the extended Delano family at the Algonac estate.

Franklin's father enjoyed spending time with him and found peace in the life of a country gentleman tending to his animals and riding around the property. Already in his early 60s by the time Franklin was eight years old, James was no longer as active in business as he had once been.

Off to Groton School

In September 1896, Franklin was sent to a boys-only boarding school at Groton, Massachusetts. His parents were sad to see him go, but they knew it was time to let Franklin get a proper education. The school had been founded in 1884 and included a gymnasium, tennis courts, a chapel, a boathouse, and a schoolhouse. Attendance at a private boarding school was a customary rite of passage for rich families; most of the boys there were from the same social class as Franklin.

However, Franklin was unique in that he joined the school in the third-year class, at

Franklin (above, at left) on a boat at Campobello. (below) FDR at age 10, 1892.

"A NATION THAT DESTROYS ITS SOILS DESTROYS ITSELF. FORESTS ARE THE LUNGS OF OUR LAND, PURIFYING THE AIR AND GIVING FRESH STRENGTH TO OUR PEOPLE."
—Franklin D. Roosevelt

age 14, not at age of 12 when most other boys began. It was quite a shock for Franklin, who had been under the protective wing of his mother for many years, to suddenly spend all

Memories of Sara Delano Roosevelt

BY ELEANOR SEAGRAVES,
Franklin and Eleanor Roosevelt's first grandchild

"SDR [Sara Delano Roosevelt] was as good a mother to Franklin as most mothers try to be to their children. Franklin was receptive to the discipline of both parents, as well as to their love. Living as they did, with enough money to assuage financial worry, both devoted themselves to the well-being of their only child [together]. The period was Victorian, the mores and manners mostly unquestioned, and the devotion and respect of each parent for the other, could not help but engender a healthy atmosphere for a child who was intellectually curious, and of a naturally cheerful disposition.

He may have wished for siblings, but, as it was, his time was pretty much his own even though each day was fairly well regulated to accomplish tasks—to read, study, play, ride his pony with his father, to meet other people (generally of his own class, and usually adults), to learn about wild birds of the Valley under his father's direction, and start a stamp collection. He had confidence in the life he knew and in the people around him; with an even temperament, I understand he could gently tease his mother in later childhood. By then, his father was dead, but Sara would have accepted teasing as a sign of health—as long as it stayed within the bounds of good manners!"

his days away from home and family. Still, he was able to adjust quickly to life in the simply furnished dormitory. Visits home during the school year were not encouraged, so Franklin did not see much of Hyde Park. Actually, he did have family at Groton. When he got there, he found his nephew Taddy Roosevelt (son of his half brother James) one year ahead of him. This must have been awkward for Franklin, who was sometimes teased and called "Uncle Franklin."

While at Groton, Franklin participated enthusiastically in baseball, football, rowing, and other team sports. Though he was not one of the best athletes at the school, he was competitive and not afraid to get dirty or risk injury. He set a new school record for the running high kick—eight feet and six inches. Franklin participated in other activities as well; he was a formidable member of the debate team and sang in the choir.

Every morning, Franklin awoke at 7:30 A.M. for breakfast, followed by services in the chapel, and then classes. Dinner was followed by another service in the chapel. The goal of schools like Groton was to prepare teenagers for college by giving them a background in the basics such as math and literature, while providing them with knowledge of Greek, Latin, German, and French languages. Groton kids were also expected to develop a strong sense of religion. Franklin was heavily influenced by the Reverend Endicott Peabody, the school's headmaster. In fact, Franklin kept in touch with Peabody long after he graduated.

In his first letter home after arriving at Groton, Franklin wrote to his "Mommerr and Popperr" that he was "getting on finely both mentally and physically." During his time at Groton, he wrote often to his parents and other relatives, who sent him a variety of presents such as grapes, a manicure case, a red sweater, ice skates, a Bible, a prayer book, and a watch. Once his Aunt Annie Lyman Hitch sent him a package containing several pounds of delicious figs, oranges, dates, and gingersnaps, which he promptly ate.

In his letters home, Franklin wrote mostly about his athletic activities, including the scores of games he played in and how he performed. He was always physically active, highly enthusiastic about sports, and full of team spirit. In one game, "the most absurd game" he ever saw, his football team beat Brookline High School by a score of 50–0. Franklin was also doing well in his studies. In May 1897, he wrote home to tell his parents that he had received the third-highest marks in his class. He finished his first school year fourth out of 17 students.

In June 1897, Franklin's cousin Theodore came up for a visit and entertained Franklin with stories about his job as the police commissioner of New York City. Theodore Roosevelt, also known as Teddy, invited Franklin to spend July 4 at his home in Oyster Bay. Franklin spent the remainder of that summer at Hyde Park and Campobello Island. While at Campobello, he made the most of the open waters, taking the 21-foot boat his father gave him on many sailing adventures in the Bay of Fundy. One time, he and a friend sailed to Grand Manan Island in search of a lost treasure rumored to have been buried there by the infamous pirate Captain William Kidd. They dug for hours, and found a plank with the initials "W. K." carved in it, but apparently this was just a false lead, because they uncovered nothing further.

In 1898, the Spanish-American War broke out. The United States sent troops to the Philippines and to Puerto Rico. The teenaged Franklin was enthralled by the war, and was seized with a desire to leave school and join the navy at a recruiting station in Boston. He and a friend saved up some money and devised a plan to sneak out of Groton hiding in the cart of the local pie man. They would then hurry to the nearest place of enlistment and join the navy. The day of the escape finally arrived, and both Franklin and his co-conspirator found themselves suddenly very sick with the measles, rather than on

Franklin at Groton School, 1897.

their way to Cuba. In fact, during his time at Groton, Franklin also contracted scarlet fever and the mumps. The close contact with dozens of other students made diseases spread rapidly. When Franklin had scarlet fever, he was quarantined with other boys who also had the disease. Franklin's out-of-bed shenanigans only prolonged his illness. Though no visitors were allowed, Franklin's determined mother climbed a ladder and stood at the top so she could see her son and talk with him through the window.

Harvard Bound

When Franklin graduated from Groton in June 1900, he felt a mixture of joy and sadness. He'd been accepted at Harvard University in Cambridge, Massachusetts, and he was glad to be moving on, yet he was sad to leave familiar surroundings. He was happy that his roommate would be Lathrop Brown, his friend from Groton School. In his first semester at Harvard, Franklin took classes in French, Latin, English literature, European history, government, and geology. Just a month after arriving at Harvard, Franklin tried out for the well-respected college newspaper the *Harvard Crimson*. He hoped that with enough hard work he would eventually become an editor. One of the first stories he wrote was a front-page scoop about Teddy Roosevelt coming to Harvard to lecture.

Franklin was very social at Harvard and joined many clubs on campus. He was voted secretary of the Freshman Glee Club, and became a member of the Yacht Club, the Hasty Pudding Club, the Fly Club, and the Political Club. Franklin became the librarian for several clubs he had joined, acquiring books for their collections.

While he was getting on well at Harvard, Franklin's family was having a tough time at home. Beginning in October 1900, Franklin's father, James, fell ill. It wasn't James's first bout of health problems. When Franklin was just seven years old, his father had a heart attack. This time his heart troubles were more serious. James's condition did not improve in November, and Franklin begged his mother to make sure his father got plenty of rest and did not overdo it. That same year, when Franklin was only 18 years old, his father died, at the age of 72. James's last will and testament instructed that his property be divided between his two sons and his widow, Sara.

Then, in September 1901, the nation was shocked by the assassination of President William McKinley, while he was visiting Buffalo, New York. Vice President Theodore Roosevelt became president upon McKinley's death, and Franklin's interest in the family history grew.

He wrote a paper titled "Roosevelts in New Amsterdam" for one of his college classes, and he asked his mother to copy for him information from the old Dutch family Bible.

During the winters of 1902 and 1903, Sara Delano Roosevelt stayed in Boston so she could be near her son. Without her husband, she was lonely and isolated in the snowy cold of Hyde Park. In January 1902, Franklin spent a few days in Washington, D.C., and was a guest at the White House at the coming-out party for President Theodore Roosevelt's daughter Alice. He called it "one of the most enjoyable and interesting three days I have ever had."

Franklin could have graduated from Harvard in three years, since he completed all his course requirements in that time, but he chose to stay on an extra year so he could be the chief editor of the *Harvard Crimson*. He had risen quickly at the newspaper. By his second year, he was assistant managing editor, then in the spring of 1901 he became managing editor. It was an exciting job to Franklin, and he enjoyed covering the progress of the football team.

At about this time, Franklin began to accumulate his own library of books. While at Harvard he found a good used bookstore. With guidance from the shopkeeper, he started a focused collection on ships and the sea. He had great fun selecting new additions to his growing library. By 1933, Franklin had a collection of 6,000 books and over 500 paintings and prints.

Franklin (bottom row, third from left) in a Harvard Glee Club photo.

2 A Penchant for Politics

*W*hile Franklin was busy toddling around the family mansion at Hyde Park, his distant cousin and future wife, Anna Eleanor Roosevelt, was born on October 11, 1884, in a house on 37th Street in New York City, just off fashionable Fifth Avenue. Her father was Elliott Roosevelt (1860–1894), Theodore Roosevelt's only brother (and Franklin's godfather), and her mother was Anna Hall (1863–1892), also from a prominent New York family. A younger brother named Elliott Jr. was born in 1889, and a second brother named Hall was born two years later. Eleanor's first meeting with her cousin Franklin came on a visit to Hyde Park when she was just 18 months old. Four-year-old Franklin gave her a piggyback ride around the nursery.

Eleanor's Childhood

When Eleanor was a little over two years old, her parents decided to take her on a trip to Europe. They sailed on a ship called the *Britannic*. Not long into the voyage a heavy fog descended over the ocean. Suddenly, another ship collided with the *Britannic*. Everyone on board panicked. The boat was evacuated, and Eleanor was passed, terrified, from the ship down to her father's waiting arms into a small boat. Eleanor's childhood was neither as stable nor nearly as happy and carefree as Franklin's. In fact, in many ways, she had a tragic childhood. Her mother suffered from severe headaches. As a child, Eleanor was rather serious, and her mother even occasionally called her "Granny" because of the way she carried herself. Though Eleanor adored her father, Elliott Roosevelt was a heavy drinker who spent long periods of time away from home. For all his shortcomings, he adored his daughter, and gave her the nickname "Little Nell."

Eleanor's mother died of a bacterial disease called diphtheria in 1892 at the age of 29. Eleanor and her brothers were sent to live with her maternal grandmother, Mary Hall. The next year, Eleanor's brother Elliott ("Ellie") Jr. died of a virus called scarlet fever at the age of four. Then, in 1894, Eleanor's father died from alcoholism, when Eleanor was only 10 years old. Unlike the outgoing and confident youngster Franklin Roosevelt, Eleanor Roosevelt was a quiet and somber child who often retreated into a fantasy world in her mind.

Eleanor's grandmother sent her to Europe to further her education when Eleanor was 15. Eleanor went with her Aunt Tissie Mortimer on a stay that lasted three years. Her time in Europe taught her the lighter side of life. She got to see the sights of England, France, Germany, and Italy. When she returned, she was a more mature and confident young woman.

Eleanor Roosevelt and her father, 1889.

> "PEOPLE GROW THROUGH EXPERIENCE
> IF THEY MEET LIFE HONESTLY AND COURAGEOUSLY.
> THIS IS HOW CHARACTER IS BUILT."
> —Eleanor Roosevelt

Engagement and Marriage

Though Franklin and Eleanor had conversed at a Christmas party when she was 13 years old, they did not meet again until she returned from Europe. One day in the summer of 1902, Franklin happened across Eleanor as he took a little walk from his seat on a train, heading north from New York City. He was going back to Hyde Park, and she was on her way to her grandmother's house along the Hudson River. From this chance encounter began a romance. They started seeing more of each other, and in 1903 their relationship became more serious. Franklin was enchanted by Eleanor's brooding beauty. The charming and popular FDR had not been in any serious relationships with girls until he met Eleanor.

In 1903, 21-year-old FDR asked Eleanor to marry him. She was 19 years old, and she said yes, in part because she felt the urge to hurry up and grow up. She wanted to leave her troubled childhood behind and experience marriage and motherhood. Though Franklin wanted to get married in 1904, his mother, Sara, felt he was still too young. So FDR and Eleanor waited a little longer and were finally married at the home of Eleanor's cousin in New York City, on March 17, 1905. The Reverend Peabody from the Groton School presided over the ceremony, FDR's old roommate

Lathrop Brown was the best man, President Theodore Roosevelt was there to give away his niece in marriage, and Alice Roosevelt (Teddy's daughter) was the maid of honor. Teddy Roosevelt's visit caused quite a stir in Manhattan. It seemed that after the wedding ceremony, the young couple was neglected as many of the guests were more interested in meeting the president than well-wishing the newlyweds.

FDR had entered Columbia Law School in New York in the fall of 1904, so their honeymoon was delayed until school was out for the summer. The young couple then set sail on the RMS Oceanic across the Atlantic for an extended trip to Europe. They wrote many letters to Franklin's mother. Eleanor thanked her mother-in-law for everything she did for the young couple, adding "You are always just the sweetest, dearest Mama to your children...."

Theirs was no budget tour of Europe, even though FDR was still in law school and not yet earning any money except for the trust money his father had left him. Upon arriving in London, the couple stayed in an expensive hotel suite because the hotel management thought they were part of President Theodore Roosevelt's immediate family. They also went to Paris, France, and Venice, Italy, as well as smaller cities and towns in Switzerland and Germany.

Franklin and Eleanor courting at Hyde Park.

The Roosevelts' first home (center of photo, two windows wide) on 36th Street in New York City still stands today.

Franklin enjoyed browsing through bookshops and antique stores. While in Italy, the Roosevelts bought several tapestries, a centuries-old Tintoretto painting, and an entire 3,000-book library. But the trip was not all fun for FDR. At one point, he sent a letter to his mother asking her to send a few law books so he could study for an upcoming law exam. Mainly, their trip consisted of visiting with relatives and family friends who were living or staying in Europe, going to the theater, exploring ancient churches, and enjoying the fresh air of the Alps.

Upon their return to the United States in the fall of 1905, FDR continued his studies in law school, but he was only an average student. A month after they returned, they moved into a small (12 feet wide) house on East 36th Street in New York City. Still, their home was just a few blocks away from FDR's mother Sara Roosevelt's city home. Sara called FDR and Eleanor's house "extremely simple, but very cosy."

Eleanor was not as enthusiastic about the sea as her husband, and she had felt particularly ill on the voyage home. When she continued to feel sick even after her return, she paid a visit to her doctor. He told her the reason for her malaise was that she was pregnant. The couple waited expectantly for their child to arrive, and in May 1906 Eleanor gave birth to a baby girl they named Anna Eleanor.

The next year was also eventful for the 25-year-old FDR. He passed the New York State Bar Exam, which allowed him to practice law, and in September 1907, he started his very first job, as an unpaid apprentice law clerk at a New York law firm called Carter, Ledyard, and Milburn. His value was soon recognized at the law firm, and he became managing clerk in charge of certain cases. A second child, James, was born in December 1907.

Around this time, Sara Delano Roosevelt was having a double house built on 65th Street as a present to the couple, where her son and his wife could live next door to her. Eleanor was not pleased about having no say in any of the arrangements. Franklin and Eleanor also spent more time at Hyde Park, where FDR became involved in community activities such as the volunteer fire department.

Motherhood did not come naturally to Eleanor. She later wrote in her autobiography that she had never liked little children very much. She hired a nurse to take care of the babies. Nonetheless, the family continued to grow. A son named Franklin D. Roosevelt Jr. was born in March 1909, but he died tragically in November of the same year of endocarditis (an inflammation of the heart). A son named Elliott was born next, in September 1910.

FDR Enters Politics

In 1910, Franklin made his first stab at politics. He became a delegate to the Democratic State Committee. Also that year, the leader of the Dutchess County Democratic Party approached FDR and asked him if he wanted to run for the office of state assemblyman. It seemed the current assemblyman, Lewis Stuyvesant Chanler, was about to retire. FDR was enthused. But when he finally talked to the assemblyman in person, Chanler told him he was not going to retire after all; however, there was an opening to run for New York State senator and FDR was welcome to try.

Franklin thought about it. The state senate was not a position of immense power, but it could be a stepping stone to a higher position. FDR decided to give it a shot, even though he had not lived at Hyde Park full time for years, and was somewhat out of touch with local politics and issues. The biggest obstacle was that the district was heavily Republican; for over 30 years Republicans had held the assembly seat for that district. It would certainly be an uphill battle. A win could kick-start his political career, but a loss could put it to a quick end. How long would FDR have to wait for another invitation from the Democratic Party, if he refused this one? He was nominated on October 6, 1910, and accepted the invitation, saying, "I am pledged to no man; I am influenced by no specific interests, and so I shall remain."

FDR began to campaign, a bit unsteadily at first. He did not yet have the knack of giving speeches and campaigning. He raised over $2,000 for his campaign, but much of it came from his mother. Slowly but surely, FDR made inroads with the local people. He and the local candidate for U.S. Congress, Richard Connell, campaigned together in the large district in one of the few cars to be had in the entire area. The striking red Maxwell roadster covered a lot of ground. They sometimes made up to 20 speeches a day. One day, Connell made a stop at a schoolhouse and motioned FDR to follow him inside. Once inside the schoolhouse, Connell asked the teacher if he could make a little speech on patriotism to the students. After he got permission, he went ahead and gave a talk to the youngsters. On the way out, FDR questioned him. Why would he want to make a speech here, in front of an audience that was too young to vote for him? He answered quite simply, "They will be one day, and then they will remember me."

Another time, the two spent an afternoon hard at work campaigning on the road, shaking hands and introducing themselves to people, only to find out that they had crossed the state line into Connecticut and had wasted

"BE SINCERE; BE BRIEF; BE SEATED."

—Franklin D. Roosevelt

the afternoon on people who were not even in their state, let alone their election district.

FDR's opponent, Republican senator John Schlosser, was fairly confident he would win. Yet, when Election Day came to a close, Roosevelt came out 1,140 votes ahead. He had done the impossible and won the election! Roosevelt and his family rented out their New York City house and moved to Albany, New York, in order to be in the state capitol. They arrived on January 1, 1911, and that same day had a large party at their house to celebrate. Franklin quit Carter, Ledyard, and Milburn, but he joined a new firm called Marvin, Hooker, and Roosevelt (though he was not an active partner).

Party Politics

In January 1911, not long after FDR had been sworn in to his new position in state government, there arose a power struggle within the New York State Democratic Party. The problem was a powerful faction of the party called Tammany Hall, known for decades for its corrupt and powerful grip over New York City politics. Since 1902, Tammany Hall had been led by a strong-willed saloon owner and politician named Charles "Boss" Murphy. Boss Murphy wanted his choice, William "Blue-Eyed Billy" Sheehan, to become the next U.S.

senator for New York State, replacing the outgoing senator Chauncey Depew. In those days, the state legislature got to choose senators; they were not chosen directly by popular vote. Unfortunately, in Sheehan's case, there was no room for discussion.

FDR was not pleased with the idea that he had to do what he was told. After all his hard work campaigning to win an unlikely victory, he did not wish to be simply a puppet. FDR began to mount an opposition to Sheehan, whom he felt was not the right choice. In his eyes, Sheehan was just another corrupt product of the Tammany Hall machine, which had been crooked for decades. So FDR had fellow assembly members over to his house, and they talked about the situation through the dense haze of cigar smoke. A local newspaper described how the "little group of insurgents" led by Franklin D. Roosevelt "dared to resist the domination of the Tammany boss."

Roosevelt even invited Sheehan to his house for a personal meeting over lunch. Roosevelt and Sheehan spoke for nearly three hours, while Eleanor entertained Mrs. Sheehan. But Sheehan would not be convinced to drop out of the running. Sheehan and his supporters told the insurgents, including FDR, that they had better give in or their careers would soon be over. FDR held fast to his beliefs. He would not give in. Slowly, FDR gained momentum

ENTERING POLITICS IS an interesting experience that can teach you a great deal about yourself, and about other people. Franklin Roosevelt was inexperienced and a bit awkward in his earliest campaign and speeches in 1910, but by the time he ran for president 22 years later, he was a seasoned political veteran. In this activity you will mount a campaign to run for class president or student council representative or some other office.

YOU'LL NEED
★ Notebook
★ Pen or pencil
★ Poster board
★ Colored markers
★ Computer (optional)
★ Glue stick (optional)
★ Photo of yourself (optional)

Who in your class would like to run for class president or any other positions you can think of? Everyone should be eligible to run and raise their hand to be nominated and run for office. After the candidates have come forward, each should prepare a short speech and a campaign slogan and posters. Those running for office should each select a campaign manager or two to help them come up with creative campaign ideas.

The first step in mounting a campaign is to have a brainstorming session. Get together with your campaign manager and other friends and come up with ideas for your speech and slogan. Think about what makes you a strong candidate and what you will do once you are elected. Your slogan should be short and catchy. In past campaigns, people have used the candidates' names and rhymed them with positive words and made playful puns using their names, or created other catchy phrases to sell their candidate. Sometimes a candidate's platform (what they are promising to do once elected) can be worked into the slogan, for example: "Vote for Jack and Bring Recess Back!" Slogans can be used to tell people about your leadership qualities. For example, one of FDR's campaign slogans was "A Gallant Leader."

Next, work on your poster. You can use colorful markers on poster board or a computer with a color printer to write out your slogans. You might want to put a picture of yourself, along with some of your campaign promises, on your poster. You can draw pictures to make your poster colorful and appealing. Your teacher will tell you where you can hang up your posters.

On Election Day, each candidate should make a speech. Your speech should be short and to the point. Be sure to speak loudly and clearly and make eye contact with your classmates when you deliver your speech. Have your poster next to you but don't stand behind it. You want to appear confident and deliver a clear message. In your speech begin by introducing yourself and talking about what makes you a good candidate. Tell the class what you hope to accomplish. Your ideas should be realistic. Don't promise something you can't deliver, like fewer school days. Ideas might include new recess activities, a class pet, homework help, better books for the classroom library, and more class parties.

When everyone is finished with their speeches, classmates should cast their votes on paper and pass the folded sheets of paper to the teacher to count them. After the votes have been tallied by the teacher, she or he should announce the winners of the election.

for the anti-Sheehan movement. Tammany finally gave in, and a compromise was reached. FDR told a local newspaper that he did not yet know who the senator would be, but he did know one thing—it would not be Sheehan. A different, less controversial candidate would be put forth. FDR insisted he did not do this to get his name in the paper, but as a "matter of principle and party policy." The Democrats, and especially Tammany, took notice of the feisty young politician with the famous name.

Building a Political Career

Eleanor now had considerable help in taking care of their three young children in the household that was often the scene of political wrangling in those early months in Albany. Six servants, including a nanny and a governess, helped the Roosevelts. FDR settled into his job, with newly won respect (and perhaps a little fear) on the part of his colleagues.

Though his days of carefree exploration in the Hyde Park woods were over, FDR's love for the outdoors was still strong. While state senator, he served as chair of the Forest, Fish, and Game Committee and was a member of the Canals, Railways, and Agriculture Committee. He tried to be a good senator and listen to what his constituents (the people who lived in his district) wanted. One time, he received a large number of postcards from people who did not want a certain bill to be passed. FDR happened to strongly support the bill. He did not know what to do. His job was to reflect the voters' wishes, but he felt this was a little unfair. It was clear to him that the postcard campaign had been an organized attempt to influence him. So FDR organized his own campaign in support of the bill. Soon enough, he received many postcards in favor of the legislation. Now he could support the bill with a clear conscience.

Though state matters were first in his mind, FDR was beginning to think on a bigger scale. He was an early supporter of Woodrow Wilson, the governor of New Jersey who was mobilizing support for a run for president. They spent time together in the fall of 1911, and the two got along well. FDR organized a group called the New York State Wilson Conference to gain support for Wilson. The Democratic National Convention was exciting in 1912, and FDR was in attendance to try to get Wilson nominated. A man named Champ Clark led in the early balloting, but Woodrow Wilson was finally nominated, thanks in part to the support FDR had given him.

As his first term drew toward a close, FDR was not sure he wanted to run again. A rumor that "Boss" Murphy did not want him to run may well have changed FDR's mind. But then FDR was stricken with typhoid fever and so could not do much campaigning for his reelection to the state senate. He called upon a friendly Albany newspaper reporter named Louis McHenry Howe to run the campaign for him. Howe had watched FDR's career and had written a favorable article on FDR. With Howe on his team, FDR now had expert advice to follow. As part of the campaign strategy, FDR took out full-page advertisements in newspapers. He won back his seat by 1,700 votes.

After Woodrow Wilson won the presidency in the 1912 election, he tried to repay those who had supported him by finding positions for them in his administration. The newly named secretary of the treasury, William Gibbs McAdoo, offered FDR the position of assistant secretary of the treasury, but that did not interest him much. He was also offered the job of collector of the port of New York, but was not interested in that either. Then, by chance, FDR ran into Josephus Daniels, the man that Wilson had selected as the secretary of the navy. Daniels already knew a little bit about FDR and was impressed. When Daniels asked if he would like to be the assistant secretary of the navy, FDR said yes in an instant. Coincidentally, his cousin Theodore had held the exact same position in 1897, and FDR would even be sitting at the very same desk his cousin had 15 years earlier. Now FDR gave up the state senate seat he had just won, and the Roosevelts moved into a pleasant house owned by Eleanor Roosevelt's aunt Bamie on N Street in Washington, D.C.

Josephus Daniels (second from left), Woodrow Wilson (third from left), and FDR (far right).

1913–1921

FDR in 1913.

The 31-year-old Franklin Roosevelt was sworn in to his new position in March 1913. Among Franklin's new duties were visiting and inspecting naval bases and ships around the country. Since he had had a passionate love of ships since childhood, this was a pleasant and interesting job for him. He not only got to inspect battleships and destroyers, he also got to ride on them. FDR tried hard to prove he was the right man for the job. He believed that the navy had to be prepared for war at any time, and strongly felt that the naval fleet was outdated and ill prepared. There were not enough battle-ready ships, and the navy department was poorly organized. FDR urged for the creation of a naval "reserve" of 50,000 men, who could be called upon in a time of war. These men could include people with knowledge of sailing and ships. With Daniels's help, Roosevelt helped reorganize the navy and make it more efficient. He was not a typical politician. He did not seem to care if his actions rubbed people the wrong way, so long as he felt he was doing the right thing. In early 1914, for example, Roosevelt stated flat out, "The navy is not fit for war." He also sponsored swimming contests among the sailors, to help prevent accidental drownings. Before long, Assistant Secretary Roosevelt had everyone's respect.

Meanwhile, Eleanor had to practice her social skills. In Washington, she visited with the wives of major Washington figures, including senators, Supreme Court justices, and members of the House of Representatives. She also received visitors in their home. Evenings, she and her husband often attended parties. It was a whirlwind social schedule, and Eleanor found it necessary to hire a secretary to assist her with coordinating her social duties. In addition, by the end of 1913, Eleanor was pregnant again, with their fourth child. A boy was born to the Roosevelts in May 1914. They named him Franklin Delano Roosevelt Jr.

Cup of Joe

BY ADELAIDE DOUGLAS KEY,
granddaughter of Josephus Daniels, secretary of the navy

"The phrase 'cup of Joe' originated with Josephus Daniels. He took away grog [alcohol] rations in the navy, and all you could have was a cup of coffee, which they called a cup of Joe after him. To the day Roosevelt died, he called Josephus Daniels 'Chief.'"

⇒ Build a Model Ship

FROM THE TIME he was young, Franklin Roosevelt had an interest in all things naval, especially in ships. He continued to collect and build model ships even as president. Model ships can vary greatly in size and complexity. The most intricate models can take many months to complete. Each tiny part must be assembled in the proper order, and painted to look accurate. Franklin had the patience and skill needed for this hobby. Do you? In this activity, you'll build a very simple model boat.

Adult supervision required

YOU'LL NEED
* 2 pounds modeling clay (type that will dry and harden without heat, such as Crayola Model Magic)
* Butter knife
* Wooden dowel (diameter ¼ inch or less, at least 15 inches long)
* Small, fine-toothed handsaw
* Sandpaper (medium and fine grain)
* Hobby paints (various colors)
* Small paint brush
* Piece of 10 × 10-inch white cotton fabric (from a T-shirt, for example)
* Scissors

* Needle
* Thin string or yarn (15 inches)
* Modeling cement or glue

Shape the clay into an oval about 6 inches long and 3 inches wide at the widest point in the center. Use the butter knife to cut the oval in half lengthwise. Take one half, cut it widthwise across the center, then put it aside. Hold

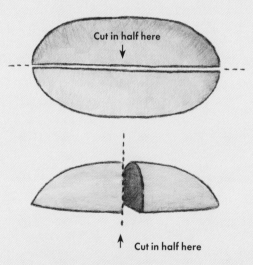

Cut in half here

↑ Cut in half here

the other piece flat side up. This is called the hull of the ship. With your thumb and forefinger, pinch the front of the hull (the bow) gently so it comes to a point. Continue gently pinching down from the front tip of the flat part (the deck)

to the underside of the boat. This slight ridge is the keel of the boat, providing stability in the water (hence the phrase "an even keel"). Continue until you create a point at the back of the hull (the stern).

Have an adult cut a 6-inch, a 3-inch, and a 2-inch length of dowel with a handsaw. Insert one of them into the center of the deck, about 1 inch deep. Remove the dowel, and set all three pieces aside.

Let the clay hull dry and harden completely, then use the sandpaper (first medium and then fine grain) to smooth the edges of the bottom. Pick a color for the bottom and a different color for the deck, and paint the hull.

Cut the fabric into two triangles: the first 4 × 3 × 5 inches (sail 1), and the second 4 × 2 × 4½ inches (sail 2). These are your two sails. Use the needle to poke four holes in each sail, about ¼

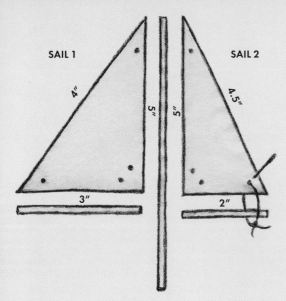

SAIL 1

4"

5"

3"

SAIL 2

4.5"

5"

2"

mast (the 6-inch dowel), and lay the sail apparatus down to dry.

Place a drop of glue into the dowel hole that you made in the hull, and insert the sail apparatus. Allow to dry. Your boat is done! Now use the two quarters of the oval piece of clay as holders (one placed on each side of the ship model) to help display the model ship and keep it on an even keel.

inch from the edge of the right-angle sides of each sail, two per side (one at each corner).

Thread a 3-inch length of string through each hole. Tie the 3-inch side of sail 1 to the 3-inch dowel, and the 4-inch side of the same sail to the top of the 6-inch dowel. There will be about 2 inches of dowel left below the sail. To the other side of the 6-inch dowel, tie sail 2's 4-inch side, and to the 2-inch dowel, tie the short (2-inch) edge of sail 2. Glue the short dowels to the main

Shortly thereafter, in the summer of 1914, World War I broke out in Europe. Though the United States had not yet entered the war, things got hectic for the armed forces. In one letter of August 1914, Franklin told Eleanor of the "strenuous days" and three nights at work until nearly 3 A.M.

In fall 1914, FDR declared his interest in being a Democratic candidate for U.S. senator. He juggled his duties in the Wilson administration with campaigning across New York State, including Buffalo, New York City, and Plattsburgh (near the border with the province of Quebec, Canada). Primary Day proved a disappointment for FDR; he lost the election to the Tammany Hall choice for senator, James Gerard. He returned to his work as assistant secretary of the navy.

In 1915, Roosevelt was present at the San Francisco World's Fair. He had the idea to kick things off with a display of naval ships from countries around the world. The exercise was a great success, with even the landlocked Switzerland and Bolivia participating.

The Roosevelt's final child, John Roosevelt, was born in March 1916. President Wilson ran for reelection in fall 1916, and on that election hinged FDR's fate. If Wilson won, there was an excellent chance Roosevelt would be kept on as assistant secretary of the navy. If Wilson lost to his Republican opponent, Charles

Evans Hughes, FDR was out of a job. Election Day 1916 was a nail-biter. Results were slow to come in, especially from California. FDR wrote of that Election Day that it was "the most extraordinary day of my life." In the end, Wilson pulled out ahead and won California, by a slim margin of 277 electoral votes to 254 electoral votes.

World War I

The Wilson administration faced new challenges in its next term. A majority of Americans wanted nothing to do with the war that was raging in Europe. They preferred a policy of isolationism, keeping the United States out of foreign affairs. However, escalating hostility by the Germans against American ships in the Atlantic Ocean led the United States to declare war on Germany on April 6, 1917, only a month after Wilson's second-term inauguration.

Roosevelt's job suddenly became even more important. In this time of war, the navy was an essential component to a victory. FDR wrote letters of thanks to Americans who donated various items to the war effort. In one case, he wrote to thank a Texas man for his donation of a platinum ring for use in munitions. The navy had a program called "Eyes for the Navy" that encouraged people to donate binoculars, telescopes, and spyglasses for use on naval ships. These were to be sent directly to Assistant Secretary Roosevelt. Upon receipt of such an item, FDR sent an official letter to each donor, saying that every effort would be made to return them after the war was won.

FDR was also responsible for helping the American navy defeat the Germans at sea. He knew that the Germans were able to clear away mines that had been laid under water pretty quickly. However, one day an inventor walked into FDR's office and showed him a new idea—metal antennas that would cause detonation of the mine (which contained 300 pounds of TNT) when brushed against a metal object such as a submarine. These were connected from the mines to the buoys that floated on the water's surface above. It would be slow going for a sub to navigate through the maze of detonator wires. FDR loved the idea and ordered 100,000 of these devices. American ships in the North Sea laid 56,000 of them. Though they were only deployed in early 1918, they were responsible for destroying or damaging about 20 submarines.

Unfortunately, FDR saw less of his family with his job as assistant secretary of the navy. The heat in Washington was stifling in July and August, so Eleanor and the children spent summers at Campobello. Franklin joined them whenever he could get away. Sometimes

FDR visiting the Brooklyn Navy Yard in New York in 1916.

the paperwork piled up and delayed him from leaving. Franklin missed his family, but he knew he had to give everything he had and do the job right.

In July 1917, Franklin wrote to his wife (then at Campobello) from Washington: "It seems years since you left and I miss you horribly. . . . I wonder how the chicks like Campo this year?" The oppressive heat and humidity of the nation's capital made him pine for the cool ocean breezes on the little island off Maine even more. One July he wrote to Eleanor that the heat "was so fierce all of last week that it just about got my goat." In another letter he wrote that he perspired all night. Despite the heat, he did manage to play golf when he could get a break. But FDR accepted political life. He felt comfortable that, between Eleanor and the domestic help, the children would be in good hands. In fall 1917, the family moved out of Aunt Bamie's house and into a larger home in Washington.

In 1918, Tammany Hall politicians offered FDR a chance to run for governor of New York State, but he declined. Because war was still raging, he felt his country needed him in the Department of the Navy. Instead, he went on a long inspection tour of American naval forces stationed in Europe beginning in July. His days were busy; he spent them traveling, meeting with officials, or inspecting naval equipment and forces. During this time, Eleanor volunteered much of her time at a Red Cross canteen in Washington, while the children spent the summer at Hyde Park with their grandmother Sara.

At the end of his European trip, Roosevelt caught a bad case of influenza, and when he finally returned home in mid-September, he was seriously sick with pneumonia. In fact, he had to be removed from the ship on a stretch-

World War I

The Great War, as it was known at the time, was triggered in June 1914 when the heir to the Austrian crown, Archduke Franz Ferdinand, was assassinated by a Serbian nationalist. Conflict had been brewing for some time among the complex cultural and political entities in Europe. After the assassination, Austria-Hungary declared war against Serbia, and Germany declared war against Russia (which supported Serbia). Before long, England, France, and Russia found themselves in a full-scale war against Germany, Italy, and Austria-Hungary. Though the United States declared its neutrality at first, the loss of 128 American lives in the sinking of the ocean liner *Lusitania* in 1915 began to stir sentiment against Germany. World War I was the first war to feature many new and deadly weapons (such as machine guns, fighter airplanes, and poison gas) and brutal trench warfare. Millions of soldiers and civilians lost their lives, and parts of France, Germany, and Belgium were laid to waste by the violence.

⇒ Decode a Navy Signal Flag Message

FRANKLIN D. ROOSEVELT was always interested in naval history. As a boy he studied naval books, and later he served as assistant secretary of the navy for eight years. Before the age of electronic radio transmissions, ships used flags with various colors and designs to communicate with other ships or with the shore. This "international language" is still used today and allows any ship to decipher a message, even if the crew members don't speak the language of the sender. During World War I and World War II, signal flags were especially important because they allowed U.S. navy and coast guard crews to communicate without using radio broadcasts, which could be intercepted by the enemy.

Each signal flag has two meanings—a letter of the alphabet as well as a short message. For example, the flag representing the letter *L* also means "stop immediately." In this activity you'll learn the letters and messages associated with each flag, and then decode a simple message.

YOU'LL NEED
★ Pen or pencil
★ Paper
★ International Signal Flags
★ Alphabet and Code Pennants

Following are a couple of examples of how a message is displayed on a ship.

If this flag were displayed by itself, it would mean "require assistance," not the letter V. But raising the letter flags for Y and Z on one flagpole means that the subsequent flags should be read as individual letters and spelled out to make words. Flags are hoisted vertically and read from top to bottom. Each word is spelled out on a separate flagpole.

(continues on next page)

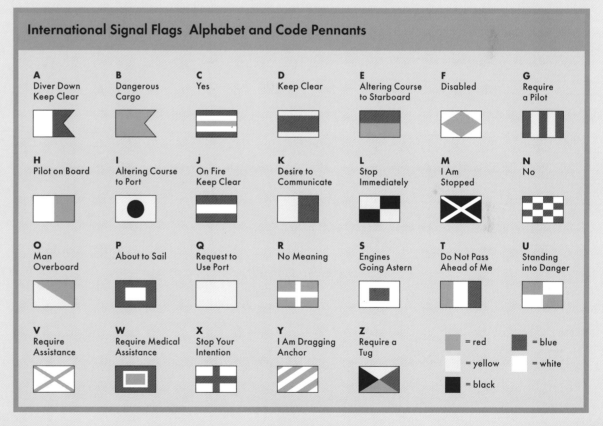

International Signal Flags Alphabet and Code Pennants

A Diver Down Keep Clear

B Dangerous Cargo

C Yes

D Keep Clear

E Altering Course to Starboard

F Disabled

G Require a Pilot

H Pilot on Board

I Altering Course to Port

J On Fire Keep Clear

K Desire to Communicate

L Stop Immediately

M I Am Stopped

N No

O Man Overboard

P About to Sail

Q Request to Use Port

R No Meaning

S Engines Going Astern

T Do Not Pass Ahead of Me

U Standing into Danger

V Require Assistance

W Require Medical Assistance

X Stop Your Intention

Y I Am Dragging Anchor

Z Require a Tug

= red
= blue
= yellow
= white
= black

This message says "READ THE FLAGS."

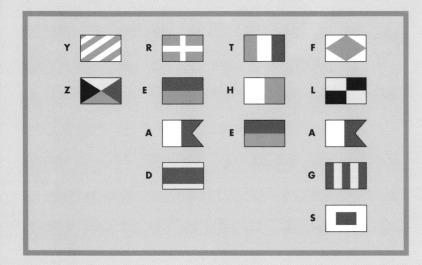

Now try decoding this spelled-out message. The answer is at the bottom of this page.

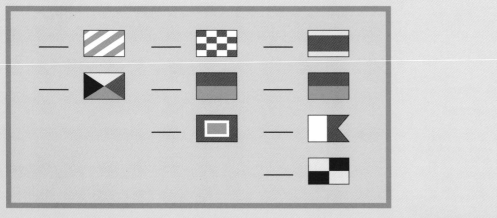

Answer: NEW DEAL

er and was not able to return to Washington until October. It was the time of the terrible global influenza epidemic that ultimately killed millions of people all over the world, and more than 500,000 in the United States alone.

The war in Europe began to turn in favor of the American, British, and French allies during the late summer of 1918, with the large influx of freshly arrived American troops facing tired German troops. It finally ended in November 1918 when Germany surrendered. FDR was sent on an extensive overseas trip in January 1919 to oversee the demobilization of naval forces in Europe. This time, Eleanor accompanied him. The children stayed home with their grandmother. While the Roosevelts sailed on the *U.S.S. George Washington*, news reached them that Theodore Roosevelt had died, at the age of 60. Eleanor wrote to her mother-in-law that they were shocked at the news. "Another big figure gone from our nation and I fear the last years were for him full of disappointment," she wrote.

President Wilson set out on a cross-country tour in September 1919 to promote a peace-keeping organization he had devised called the League of Nations. The idea of the League was to create a means for addressing conflict and avoiding war. Other countries wanted to join, but the U.S. Congress was hesitant.

After 8,000 miles and 29 cities, Wilson returned to Washington, but the United States was no closer to joining the League than before. Many people simply wished to return to isolationism. Shortly after, Wilson had a severe stroke that left him badly paralyzed.

Strained Relationship

Late in 1913, Eleanor had hired a part-time private secretary. The 22-year-old woman's name was Lucy Mercer. Tall and elegant, young Lucy was from a well-established

FDR and his family in 1919. From left to right: Anna, FDR Jr., FDR, Elliott, Eleanor, James, Sara Delano Roosevelt, and John.

Teddy Roosevelt (TR) Versus Franklin Delano Roosevelt (FDR)

BY KERMIT ROOSEVELT,
great-grandson of President Theodore Roosevelt

"Most of my immediate family leans Democratic. Growing up, I viewed FDR as a great president. My parents told me that in previous generations there had been some tension between the FDR and TR wings of the family, but that really doesn't exist anymore—I've been to a couple of reunions where everyone got along quite happily.

I always say that I'm not entirely sure what it means to be a Roosevelt because I have no experience being anything else. For me, it means that I have a sense that it's possible to contribute to society, and that I should try to. FDR and TR are inspirational in that both of them overcame great difficulties—FDR's polio, and TR's early loss of his wife and mother—on the way to their successes. They're also daunting if you think that you have to live up to their examples, but all I ask of myself is that I make an effort."

Maryland family. After working with Lucy, Eleanor quickly grew to like the personable young woman. Lucy also got along well with the Roosevelt children. She remained an employee of the Roosevelts for several years. At times when FDR was assistant secretary of the navy, Eleanor and the children went to Cam-

pobello, and FDR stayed behind in Washington, along with Lucy Mercer. Eleanor became jealous that her husband spent so much time with Lucy. One day, the two were seen driving together in the suburbs of Washington.

In 1917, after the United States had entered World War I, Eleanor told Lucy she was no longer needed because there was not much for her to do anymore. Lucy enlisted in the navy and wound up becoming a naval secretary attached to Assistant Secretary Roosevelt's office. They still saw each other regularly. Gossip spread around Washington about Lucy and Franklin spending so much time together.

In fall 1918, when Franklin had returned from his overseas trip with pneumonia, Eleanor unpacked his bags. While emptying the contents of one of his trunks, Eleanor happened across a bundle of letters that Lucy had sent to Franklin during the trip. As she read, her heart sank. They were love letters, and it truly crushed Eleanor. Eleanor confronted Franklin. They talked about it. Eleanor offered Franklin a divorce. Sara Delano Roosevelt was firmly against this idea. FDR and Eleanor decided to stay together.

However, after the confrontation in 1918, the relationship between Eleanor and FDR was strained. Though Lucy Mercer got married in 1920, Eleanor never forgot Franklin's relationship with Lucy.

Memories of Woodrow Wilson

BY REVEREND FRANCIS B. SAYRE JR.,
grandson of President Woodrow Wilson

"I was born in the White House and am the last one to have been born in the White House. I have a vivid memory [of Woodrow Wilson] because I saw a great deal of him, since we lived not far away, just within walking distance of where he lived. I was his first grandchild. [After he left the White House], he lived just down the street, a few blocks, in his house which he owned all the time he was in the White House. That's where I got to know him the best. He was a busy man, very busy. But he enjoyed seeing his first grandchild, and I enjoyed seeing him a great deal.

We talked politics, rather than fly by night stuff. I was young and I didn't understand politics like my granddad did. But I wanted to talk with him because he was famous. And he enjoyed talking with me. One principal legacy [he left] was the League of Nations, which he was all for, and hoped we would join. [The Congress was] always behind in that issue. They didn't want to involve poor old United States in foreign countries."

Eleanor did not let herself get too emotionally close to Franklin ever again. Their relationship was never again quite as warm and loving as it had been when they were courting. They spent days and weeks apart at times. Still, they respected and supported each other. The marriage became more like a business partnership. This arrangement seemed to work. As a power couple, the Roosevelts were very successful. America loved them both.

Back on the Campaign Trail

At the Democratic National Convention held in San Francisco in August 1920, Governor James Cox of Ohio, a former newspaperman, was selected as the Democratic nominee for president. When it came time to select a running mate for Cox, FDR was one of those whose names were suggested. Governor Cox liked the idea, and FDR was nominated for vice president. The old Tammany machine could no longer stop the up-and-coming Franklin Roosevelt.

In his acceptance speech, given on the steps of his home at Hyde Park, Roosevelt expressed thanks and humility. He also spoke words that seemed to predict his future approach to government: "[W]e have been awakened

FDR on the campaign trail, 1920.

by this war into a startled realization of the archaic shortcomings of our governmental machinery and of the need for . . . reorganization." He also urged the United States to live in the modern world and realize that lives in one country have become interwoven with lives in other countries. Being isolated was no longer possible.

The presidential campaign was nothing like the campaign for state senate had been. This time, the scale was national, and the stakes were much higher. FDR campaigned tirelessly and continued to learn about the concerns of common Americans. He gave hundreds of speeches all across the country. After meeting with a frail Woodrow Wilson in the summer of 1920, FDR and Cox decided that the critical issue for the election should be Wilson's idea of a League of Nations. Cox and Roosevelt spoke out for the League, arguing that America needed to participate to ensure world peace.

It was a tiring campaign. On one day in August 1920, FDR gave five speeches in four different towns in South Dakota, and traveled 80 miles by car. During the campaign, he once again had the help of his friend Louis Howe.

The Republican candidate, Warren G. Harding, was also a former newspaperman from Ohio. The Republicans were against the League of Nations, and against the United States' involvement in the war. Harding was sure to get his views across wherever he campaigned.

The Republicans put out a series of pamphlets in which they criticized the Democrats. The Republicans claimed that the Democrats had spent $20 billion and wasted too much money on the war. In closing, one pamphlet said: "the Democratic party which perpetrated these outrages upon the American people,

Roosevelt and Harding

BY WARREN G. HARDING III,
great-nephew of President Warren G. Harding

"What [Harding] really enjoyed doing was playing golf, and he picked it up while he was the senator from Ohio, and they had a group called the Senate Foursomes. They tried to play every week during good weather there in Washington. They played at a club called Chevy Chase most of the time, and one of the members of that group was Franklin Roosevelt, while he was the assistant secretary of the navy. So people back then knew each other as people, and they respected each other for the most part. Even though they had their differences, they could get along and enjoy a game of golf, and I think they worked a lot of their political differences out on a lot more friendly basis than people tend to do today."

now has the embalmed impudence in the face of its record to call upon the nation to retain it in power and to enable it, under the mere alias of Cox and Roosevelt, to perpetuate . . . the devastating policies and practices of Woodrow Wilson's Administration."

Though Cox and Roosevelt campaigned hard, in the end, they lost. On Election Day, November 2, 1920, the Republican candidates, Warren G. Harding for president and Calvin Coolidge for vice president, won by a margin of 16 million to 9 million votes. The majority of the country preferred Harding's vision of a return to the isolationism of the pre-war era. The war years had been an exhausting and upsetting time for most Americans. They simply did not want the United States to continue to be a major player in world affairs.

Now, for the first time in 10 years, FDR was out of public office. What should he do next? He decided to do what most out-of-work politicians did—return to private sector work.

Memories of James Cox

BY ANNE COX CHAMBERS,
daughter of James M. Cox, 1920 Democratic nominee for President

"My father seldom spoke of the campaign. He was a man of the moment; always living in the present and looking at the future, not the past. He had no regrets about losing the election and put all of his energy into developing his newspaper business. However, he maintained a warm and open relationship with Franklin D. Roosevelt until FDR's death. He was offered several high level and prestigious positions during the Roosevelt administration but turned them all down, preferring to help the nation through his media business."

"I ASK YOU TO JUDGE ME BY THE ENEMIES I HAVE MADE."

—Franklin D. Roosevelt

3 OVERCOMING ALL OBSTACLES

It was winter in New York, January 1921. Franklin Roosevelt was now 39 years old. He had moved up the political ladder from a starter position in the New York State legislature to an important position in President Woodrow Wilson's cabinet. Finally, he had been the Democratic choice for vice president. He had to wonder if this was the end or just the beginning of his political career. Would the Democrats come back to him in 1924? How long would the Republicans reign?

The Roosevelt family moved from Washington back to East 65th Street in New York City, where FDR quickly returned to private law practice as a partner in the firm Emmet, Marvin, and Roosevelt. He also took on a role as a vice president in the New York office of a company called Fidelity and Deposit. Meanwhile, the children were getting older. James Roosevelt, now a teenager, had entered Groton. The youngest child, John, was now nearly five years old.

Polio Strikes

In July 1921, Eleanor went ahead to Campobello with the children while Franklin returned to Washington to testify at a Senate hearing. The hearing was about the navy department's knowledge and handling of misbehavior during the war at the Newport, Rhode Island, naval base. Once FDR satisfied the committee that the navy department (including himself) had not shown any neglect or intentional wrongdoing, he was able to leave Washington.

Roosevelt did not go directly to Campobello, however. His first stop was Bear Mountain State Park in New York, where he visited a Boy Scout camp. At the time, he was president of the Greater New York Boy Scouts Council.

He finally rejoined the family in early August 1921. Little did he know then that what should have been a pleasant, uneventful vacation would soon turn into a nightmare and change his life. On August 10, FDR and the family were on his boat, the *Vireo*. They noticed a forest fire in the distance, and landed the boat. Franklin and his sons tried to put out the fire. Then they went for a swim in a nearby lake. Later that day FDR went for another swim, this time in the cold water of the Passamoquoddy Bay. When Franklin sat

on dry land again for about an hour after his swim, going through the large amount of mail that had accumulated for him, he felt a chill and soon decided to go to bed. He wanted to get warm and shake off what he thought was a cold coming on.

But rather than improving, his condition worsened in the morning. He now had great pain in his back and legs, and a fever as well. His right leg was weak, and he could not support his weight on it. A local doctor was called in. After examining Franklin, the doctor felt that it was just a cold.

By the evening of August 12, though, Franklin's left leg also weakened. By the morning of the 13th, Franklin could no longer walk, stand, or even move his legs. That same day, another doctor examined FDR and felt it was a blood clot that had lodged itself in FDR's spinal cord, causing him to lose feeling in his legs. For the next several days, the Roosevelts understood that FDR would take a while to recover, but they still thought he was suffering only from some type of congestion in the lower spine.

The fever lasted a full week before going away. FDR's muscles below the waist were also painfully sensitive to the touch. By August 23, Eleanor wondered if it might be a serious disease known as poliomyelitis (polio for short). They sent for a specialist from Boston, who confirmed the suspicion. FDR was suffering from polio.

As most people at the time knew, polio was a disease that struck suddenly. It was spread by contact with infected people. There had been an epidemic in 1916 in New York that had worried FDR and his family. Yet, less than one percent of all people who got polio had permanent paralysis. Polio was also most common in children under five years old, and that was why the most severe form of polio was known as infantile paralysis. Out of those people who were paralyzed, some actually died when their breathing muscles stopped working. Unfortunately, there was little anyone could do for polio. There was no cure.

The only thing that might help FDR feel better was hot baths. Under water, FDR would be able to possibly coax a little movement from his lower body. Though the specialist could not predict how severe the long-term effects would be, he did say that patients' progress depended on their outlook and determination. Eleanor was shocked when the doctor sent a bill of $1,000 for his services.

During the first weeks, FDR was helpless, reduced to lying on his back. Eleanor had to take care of him and wait on his needs. She slept on the couch in the room where he lay. He was also afraid of his children getting the disease, which was contagious for the first few

Polio

Polio was one of the most dreaded diseases of the first half of the 20th century, especially for children, who were more likely to be affected. Tens of thousands of people were infected every year in the United States, with up to a few thousand deaths reported annually. In 1952, over 30 years after FDR was afflicted, one of the worst outbreaks occurred, with 58,000 cases reported. About that time, a scientist named Jonas Salk began to test a vaccine for the disease. In 1955, widespread vaccination was performed, and within a few years, the disease was largely eradicated.

weeks. They decided not to let the newspapers know the extent of FDR's illness just yet.

Louis Howe, who had been just about to begin a new job, instead went to Campobello to help his friend Franklin. He immediately did what he knew best—assessed the situation and decided how to proceed. It was decided that FDR should leave Campobello as soon as he was able and return to New York City for better medical care. On September 13, he made the trip by train. His illness was kept from the public eye while he made the trip. When he arrived in New York, he was admitted into Presbyterian Hospital, hoping that a few weeks of therapy there would help him recover. When FDR's doctor finally announced to the world that Roosevelt had polio, he said that FDR would not be crippled.

Once the official announcement was made, FDR received many letters of support, including one from his old friends at the Washington Navy Yard and another from an 87-year-old woman who also had the disease but was able to walk with a cane.

He was released from the hospital on October 28, with his legs in plaster casts. He did not have much improvement to show for his hospital stay. He simply could not move his legs at all. Howe remained loyally by FDR's side. His mother, Sara, wanted him to lead a quiet existence at Hyde Park while he recuperated, perhaps taking some time to write books (something he had wanted to do). She was not so sure that FDR would ever recover. Yet both Eleanor and Louis Howe felt it would be better for Franklin to remain a bit more active. They both believed he still had a chance at a successful return to politics. Franklin agreed with them and moved back to the house at East 65th Street.

Warm Springs

Back at home, the rich and well-connected Franklin Delano Roosevelt, who could have had almost anything he wanted, now struggled to get his life back. He was still somewhat helpless and needed Eleanor's assistance with many daily tasks that would otherwise have been second nature.

Still, in his heart, FDR felt certain that he would walk again, and he spent much time over the next few years trying to recapture the partial use of his legs. For all of his 39 years, he had been extremely active and enjoyed all kinds of outdoor activities. It was a huge blow to suddenly be confined to a wheelchair, unable even to stand up. But FDR handled his new limits very well. He was not depressed and did not want anyone's pity. Instead he was determined to continue making his life matter. It also helped that Eleanor did not treat him like an invalid.

In February 1922, FDR was fitted with steel leg braces. These seven-pound braces went from the hips all the way down to the feet (eventually he got lighter braces). They could lock into place, allowing FDR to stand, though he had to hold on to something to keep his balance. Though the braces helped him get around, they did not help him get better. For that, he had to remove the braces and gently exercise the muscles. He learned that it was important not to let his legs get cold.

During those first years of recovery, FDR worked from home much of the time. He hired a secretary named Marguerite "Missy" LeHand who came to his home and helped with his work. LeHand would go on to serve FDR for many years and become his close friend and confidant. While recovering, FDR often received visitors in the morning from his bed. He was determined not to be useless.

FDR rented a houseboat in 1923 and took a trip to Florida for a change of scenery and to try to improve his health. In 1924, he and a friend bought a houseboat. Later that year, during his continuing search for a cure, someone told FDR about a place called Warm Springs, Georgia. This run-down resort featured natural springs that were rich with mineral salts. The property had an old three-story hotel along with a few guest cottages. After that first six-week visit in 1924, FDR was impressed with what he felt was the healing power of the warm mineral water on his leg muscles. He felt that he had made great progress in just a short amount of time. Reporters tracked FDR down with an interest in his comments on the 1924 election, and one story mentioned Warm Springs.

By 1924, the buoyant effect of the water helped FDR stand up in shoulder-deep water without the use of leg braces. He noted that as time passed, he could stand in slightly more shallow water—first chin-deep, then shoulder-deep, then in water that went up to his armpits.

When FDR returned to Warm Springs in April 1925, he saw that the article that mentioned Warm Springs had prompted other polio sufferers to visit. People had heard of his progress and began to make the pilgrimage there. He was pleased to see this, but he also realized that the current Warm Springs facility was in no shape to handle many visitors.

By March 1926, FDR had actually thrown $200,000—two-thirds of his fortune—into buying Warm Springs. He eventually created the Georgia Warm Springs Foundation, a non-profit group dedicated to raising money for the resort. One of the most well known contributors to the foundation was automobile maker Henry Ford's son Edsel, who donated money for a new indoor pool.

FDR had a grand plan to turn Warm Springs into a world-class health spa and resort. As overseer of the foundation, FDR even worked closely with an architect to help design the cottages that were on site for patients. Ever proud of his heritage, FDR told the architect he wanted some Dutch touches in the design of the buildings. When the architect showed him the plans, Franklin insisted that a window arch was not Dutch. The architect insisted it absolutely was—Pennsylvania Dutch. Franklin laughed and explained to the architect that the Pennsylvania Dutch were actually German, not Dutch.

FDR fishing in Florida, 1926.

FDR swimming at Warm Springs.

who had good experiences and so came back every year.

Always wishing to make things better, FDR wanted to get corporations to send people who were recovering from injuries to Warm Springs for treatment. He gave the example of a corporation giving a gift of $30,000, which would pay for treatment for 10 of its ailing employees at Warm Springs. By 1930, his vision was becoming a reality, as 30 patients with ailments other than polio were treated at Warm Springs.

FDR was very proud of the growth at Warm Springs. He wrote in 1931, "There is always a great deal of satisfaction in observing growth and progress. As each year goes by I derive special pleasure from reading Dr. Hubbard's interesting report [an annual report about the status of Warm Springs] indicating an ever widening field of service at Warm Springs to paralysis patients."

FDR had created a special atmosphere where polio patients could meet and work to improve their health. He had a little cottage of his own there, where he later had an office.

At Warm Springs, FDR was humble and caring. He mingled with the patients, talked to them, and raised their spirits. He genuinely enjoyed helping the polios, as sufferers of polio were sometimes called. FDR's dream for Warm Springs was coming true.

Under FDR's guidance, the number of patients treated at Warm Springs grew. In 1928, 151 patients were treated; in 1929 there were 215 patients, and in 1930 there were 248 patients. Many of these were return patients

The Slow Road Back to Politics

Meanwhile, Franklin took a small step toward reentering politics. Before his illness, he had hoped to run for president again in 1924. Though Louis Howe explored this possibility a bit, there was now no serious intention on FDR's part. He knew it was too soon. He wished he could throw away his crutches and walk again. Ever the optimist, he hoped that would happen soon. In the meantime, FDR smartly chose to head the New York Alfred Smith for President Committee. Democrat Alfred Smith was the governor of New York at the time. FDR knew he needed all the Democratic friends he could find—friends who might help him gain political office down the road. As head of the committee, FDR helped organize campaign events for the candidate and rally support within New York State. Franklin was eventually chosen to make the nominating speech for Alfred Smith at the 1924 Democratic National Convention in New York City. It had been four years since FDR had had to give a speech this important.

When it was his time to speak, FDR walked to the podium from his seat using crutches and assisted by his son James. He made it about 15 feet with only his crutches as his son watched

⇒ Be Charitable

HELPING OTHER PEOPLE who had polio was one of FDR's passions. Besides money, he gave his time and compassion to those who were afflicted with this disease and to others who were paralyzed. Polio has been mostly eradicated thanks to the polio vaccine, but there are other ailments that affect many children today such as juvenile diabetes, childhood leukemia, and paralysis as a result of injury. In this activity, you will raise money for the March of Dimes, one of FDR's favorite charities.

YOU'LL NEED
- ★ Pencil
- ★ Dime
- ★ Foam board, 30 × 40 inches
- ★ Marker
- ★ Computer and printer (optional)
- ★ Double-sided tape or washable glue

Using the pencil, copy a large outline of FDR's profile from a dime onto the foam board. When you have got it right, use the marker to trace it. At the top, write neatly in thick letters "FDR Helps the March of Dimes" and the name of your group (for example, Harrison High School). Your goal is to collect enough dimes to fill in FDR's profile completely with dimes.

You will need to promote your idea among your friends, schoolmates, and family members. You can design, print out, and distribute flyers with your charity's name and a few words about your mission and plan. Ask for volunteers or donations, and include information about where your group can be reached. If people don't have dimes, you can collect other coins or bills then take them to the bank and convert them to dimes. As you get dimes, use small pieces of double-sided tape (or even washable glue) to secure the dimes to the foam board. When you have filled in FDR's portrait with dimes, go to www.marchofdimes. com to find the nearest location where you can present your donation. If there is no nearby office, you can photograph your board, then cash in the dimes, have an adult write a check, and mail the check along with the photo and a note.

proudly. In a powerful speech, FDR referred to Governor Smith as "the happy warrior of the political battlefield." Despite FDR's strong speech, in the end, Smith was not nominated. A lawyer named John W. Davis was nominated after a long and drawn-out process. Still, Smith and the Democratic party never forgot the powerful speech. It put FDR back in the public spotlight, if only momentarily, as a reminder that he had not disappeared completely from the political scene. Just a few days after the speech, one newspaper called Roosevelt "the real hero" of the convention.

After his unsuccessful convention, Alfred Smith decided to run for reelection as governor of New York that November. Ironically, he ran against the Republican Theodore Roosevelt Jr., and won. Also in November 1924, the Democratic nominee for president, John W. Davis, lost badly to the Republican Calvin Coolidge, 15 million to 8 million votes. FDR realized that, nationally, the Democratic Party was not in very good shape. He wondered what could be done to reverse the trend, now that the Democrats had lost two presidential elections in a row.

Wishing to do something to help the Democrats, FDR sent a letter to 3,000 party leaders all over the country, urging more frequent communication between the national party leaders and the leaders within each state, and early planning for the next election. In 1925, FDR tried to organize a national conference for the Democrats to talk about their plans and strategies, but the Democrats were still not a united group.

Though he still kept a watchful eye on politics, a discouraged FDR now mostly concentrated on his business interests. In 1925, Franklin started a law firm of his own, with a young partner named Basil O'Connor (who also became involved with Warm Springs, serving on the foundation's board). FDR enjoyed work at Roosevelt and O'Connor. He continued to visit Warm Springs regularly and felt some improvement in his legs. He was soon able to drive a specially equipped car. In fact, between Florida, Warm Springs, and other getaway spots, FDR spent a great deal of time out of New York State and away from his family during his recovery. During this time he also remained active in many organizations. He was the chairman of the New York branch of the American Legion Endowment Fund, a trustee of Vassar College, president of the American Construction Council, and president of the Taconic State Park Commission. FDR tried to get in the newspaper headlines occasionally and keep up his political profile.

In 1928, Franklin remained a champion of Alfred Smith, who was campaigning again for president, and this time Smith was nominated at the convention in Houston, Texas. FDR was pleased with the way the convention went, and his nominating speech was again covered very favorably in the press. This time, FDR was able to walk into the convention hall without crutches. He now used a cane, and held on to the arm of his son Elliott.

Eleanor Becomes Politically Active

During FDR's absence from politics, Eleanor Roosevelt had herself become politically active. She had already done some volunteer work for the Red Cross and the League of Women Voters. Now she joined the Women's Trade Union, became involved in the women's division of the Democratic State Committee of New York, and joined several other clubs and organizations. She also began to make speeches at various events. In 1928, Eleanor worked on Alfred Smith's campaign for president, making speeches and appearances on behalf of FDR.

Eleanor had become a more independent woman over the years, first after her last child was out of his infancy, and then more so after FDR's illness. One summer, she decided to take Franklin Jr. and John on a camping trip while Sara Delano Roosevelt took Anna and

James to Europe. Also with them were two other children—Eleanor's nephew Henry and a family friend, George Draper. They traveled up near Albany, on to Montreal, Canada, and then to Quebec City, on to the White Mountains of New Hampshire, and on through to Maine and Campobello.

FDR in his car at Hyde Park, 1928.

Governor Roosevelt

In April 1928, FDR wrote to his mother that he did not anticipate having any pressing business after September 1. While Roosevelt himself had few plans for the immediate future, Alfred Smith wanted him to become the next governor of New York. When the possibility was offered to him, FDR was not terribly enthusiastic about it, and his mother felt FDR was not quite ready to get back into the active political life. In July he told his mother that he would reject a nomination for governor. In September, he did turn Alfred Smith down. Letters and telegrams littered his desk, asking that he run.

Alfred Smith would not give up. The most powerful New York Democrats felt that if FDR ran for governor of New York, it would help Smith win New York State's electoral votes and give him a better shot at the presidency. On October 1, FDR again turned Smith down. It was getting late. The Democrats needed a candidate. Smith called FDR again and pleaded. He told FDR it was his duty to run and carry on the great progress the Smith administration had made in the past several years. The candidate for lieutenant governor even offered to cover for FDR when he needed to be at Hyde Park. In the end, Smith's pleading wore FDR down. He reluctantly accepted and was nominated on October 2.

Surprisingly, the statewide campaign invigorated Roosevelt. He worked hard, crisscrossing thousands of miles all over New York by automobile. He listened carefully to what people had to say to him, whether they were small-town Democratic leaders or ordinary people. The Franklin Roosevelt of 1928 was different from the young man who had run for vice president in 1920. He had been humbled by his illness, and he had spent time with the common people. His speeches reflected this new perspective.

After the polls closed on Election Day, FDR heard that presidential candidate Smith had lost New York State, which had the largest number of electoral votes of any state. FDR was certain that as a fellow Democrat he would suffer a similar fate. In fact, it barely crossed his mind that the governorship was possible without Smith winning the state. A tired and dejected Franklin went home, but his mother did not give up. She remained at campaign headquarters, hoping that a miracle would occur. After all, election returns were still coming in from upstate districts. Just before dawn, it was declared official: Roosevelt had pulled ahead by 25,000 votes and won the election. It was too late even to make it into the morning newspapers, which mistakenly proclaimed Roosevelt's loss.

Nationally, Smith was also defeated. This time, the Republican Herbert Hoover won the presidency. Though Alfred Smith was quite depressed about his loss, he soon put all his energy into helping FDR transition into his new position as governor. Between November and the inauguration in January, Smith talked a great deal to FDR and gave him some suggestions for people to use in his administration. Although he respected Smith a great deal, FDR did not always agree with his suggestions. FDR realized that he needed a fresh start in certain areas and wanted to be governor on his own terms.

When he was inaugurated, he first thanked Smith, whom he called "a public servant of true greatness." He then expressed his hope that his time in office would be known as an "era of good feeling." He threw himself wholeheartedly into his work as governor. FDR had seen the people of the state and felt he had a good grasp of what kinds of programs and legislation the state needed. He worked hard, coming up against a Republican-run state legislature.

The governor's mansion needed a few alterations to accommodate its new resident. FDR had a terrible fear of being trapped in a fire, not only because he was paralyzed, but also because his Aunt Laura Delano had burned to death when he was only a toddler. An elevator and ramps were installed. In addition, an outdoor pool was built for FDR to soak in.

Once in office, Roosevelt got busy. The single biggest issue in the campaign had been developing the great potential of using the waterpower of the St. Lawrence River (on the border with Canada) to supply electricity. The Republicans favored letting private companies develop and supply electricity. Roosevelt and the Democrats preferred that the state be in charge. "The water power of the State should belong to all the people," FDR said. He did not want to see the issue "delayed by petty squabbles" any longer.

Governor Roosevelt in the State Capitol Building, Albany, New York, 1930.

After FDR had been in office for a year and a half, the stock market crashed in October 1929. The stock market crash shocked the entire nation. It set off a frenzy of worried people selling off their stocks, trying to cash in before their stocks became worthless. Still, at first, nobody was certain whether the economic downturn was temporary or would last much longer. In fact it was the beginning of a long economic slump that would take hold of the nation and leave millions of people jobless and penniless. This slump was soon to be known as the Great Depression.

Governor Roosevelt saw unemployment rising in his state and decided to do something about it. But analyzing facts and figures was not personal enough. FDR visited a sweater mill and talked to the owner and the workers. He got a feel for their dire situation and understood the big picture. The once prosperous mill had been forced to accept an order for very cheap sweaters. The mill owner was desperate. He knew that the people buying sweaters could not afford to pay pre-Depression prices. There were no other orders coming in. There was no choice for the mill owner, or for the workers. The workers were being paid less to work longer hours, and the owner was barely scraping by, not making any profit out of the deal. With that visit, it was easy for FDR to understand the real effects of the Depression—when people had no money to spend, it affected the whole economy.

FDR did not feel that President Hoover was doing a very good job at managing the Depression. But for the moment, that was not his problem. His concern was to do what he could for New York. Governor Roosevelt created the Commission on the Stabilization of Employment, which looked into ways to help the situation. He even invited governors of neighboring states to a three-day conference on unemployment. It was during this time that FDR first saw the need for unemployment insurance, an issue he would later push as president.

The Great Depression

The economy of the 1920s was so strong that the era became known as the Roaring Twenties. If it seemed too good to be true, it was. Everything came to a sudden end on "Black Tuesday," October 29, 1929. The stock market crashed, meaning that stock prices for many hundreds of companies plummeted, and many people's once hefty investments were suddenly worth next to nothing. The crash set off a nationwide panic and triggered a massive economic downturn that was known as the Great Depression. During the months and years following the stock market crash, banks failed and unemployment soared.

Aspiring to Higher Office

Governor Franklin Roosevelt ran for reelection in 1930 and won handily, by a margin of 725,000 votes, a huge improvement over his slim 25,000-vote lead in 1928. The people had spoken. The Democratic Party now took serious notice. By the end of 1930, one senator had already proclaimed his support for FDR in the far-off presidential race of 1932.

During his time as governor FDR began to exploit the relatively new technology of radio to get his political message across and to communicate with his constituents. In the days before television, he got in the habit of giving occasional radio addresses in which he informed people all across the large state of New York about his plans and progress.

When 1932 came around, plenty of people thought of FDR for president. Among them were Louis Howe and another early supporter of FDR, a New York State Democratic leader named James Farley. In January 1932, it was decided that the Democratic National Convention would be held in Chicago that year. On January 22, 1932, FDR officially announced that he would run for president.

This was not a simple undertaking. He would have to face a series of challenges in various states. There were many Democrats who were trying to get the nomination that

year. FDR would need to win early and often in the primary elections to get his momentum going. Unfortunately, FDR's friendship with Alfred Smith was not what it had once been. In October 1931, Smith opposed an FDR proposal for the reforestation of abandoned farms in New York State that would cost $20 million. Smith declared his interest in running again for president, and was on the ballot in New

Living room radios of the 1930s were large and often built into wooden cabinets. People gathered around them and listened to programs together.

Stage a Radio Show

RADIO RULED FROM the 1920s through the 1940s. Radio during the Depression featured all types of shows—everything from soap operas to comedies to science fiction and detective shows. The actors usually broadcast live before a studio audience. Sound effects were used to help the listeners at home imagine the scene.

A wide variety of sound effects used an array of props, including shoes (to pound on the floor to imitate someone walking), inflated balloons (to pop with a pin for gunshots), a bicycle horn (for a car horn), a nearby door (to open and close to signal when someone has entered or left the room), and a pot of water (for dripping, plopping, and splashing noises). Try your hand writing a short script and animating it with sound effects.

YOU'LL NEED
* Pen or pencil
* Notebook
* A couple of friends
* A variety of sound props (such as the items listed above, plus any others you can think of)
* Tape recorder
* Blank tape
* An audience of two or more people

Here are some ideas for characters that you could write into your script:

Police chief, a grizzled 30-year veteran who has seen it all

Police sergeant, a young woman who does not get along with the chief

Sheriff, who wants the glory of catching the crook all to himself

FBI agent, who does not trust the police

Gangster, out to take control of the town

Henchmen and women, who do the gangster's dirty work

Man or woman in distress, because his or her uncle is suspiciously missing

Narrator (the narrator begins to tell the story, before the characters start talking, and also reads the commercials)

Now write a short script featuring some of these characters or others you have invented. Make sure you place instructions for the sound effects into the script. Assign roles in the radio play to your friends and do a rehearsal. Include commercials just before the radio program, at a break in the middle, and at the end.

A commercial may go like this:

"And now a word from our sponsor. Germ-Away is the best mouthwash you can find. Kill those nasty germs that live in your mouth and make every breath sweet and refreshing. Germ-Away. Remember it's not just good for you, it's good for everyone who comes near you!"

You may want to tape record a rehearsal to see how the sound effects come out; then you can make any adjustments or corrections. When you are ready, tape the final performance and play it back for your family and friends.

Hampshire and Massachusetts. Other states followed in adding Smith to their ballots.

FDR won the New Hampshire primary on March 8 (the first Democratic primary contest of the election season) by a comfortable margin. Winning a state primary meant that FDR was assured the votes of a majority of the state's Democratic delegates. These delegates were needed to secure the nomination at the national convention later that year.

On March 15, FDR won the North Dakota primary without much trouble, and more victories followed—Maine, Iowa, Nebraska, Minnesota, and Wisconsin.

Massachusetts worried FDR's supporters the most, since Smith was thought to have great support there. FDR stayed in the race and was defeated badly. FDR won by a slight margin in Pennsylvania, but when California's primary came around, he lost again. He also lost in Connecticut and Rhode Island, but won in Florida and Oregon.

On April 7, FDR gave a speech in which he called the economic crisis in the country more serious than what the nation had faced in 1917, when it was thrust into a world war. He said that the government had to build "plans that rest upon the forgotten . . . that build from the bottom up and not from the top down, that put faith once more in the forgotten men at the bottom of the economic pyramid."

When it was time for the June 1932 Democratic convention, FDR found himself with over 50 percent of the delegates. He was close to having the two-thirds majority required.

The Roosevelt Business and Professional League was created to get business leaders involved in the 1932 Roosevelt campaign.

Telephone: VAnderbilt 3-9021 - 9022

ROOSEVELT BUSINESS AND PROFESSIONAL LEAGUE

342 MADISON AVENUE

NEW YORK CITY

President
JESSE ISIDOR STRAUS

Secretary
DWIGHT L. HOOPINGARNER

Vice-Presidents

LATHROP BROWN, N. Y.
R. M. DRUMHELLER, Wash.
GRENVILLE T. EMMET, N. Y.
EDWIN L. GARVIN, N. Y.

ELWOOD HAMILTON, Ky.
CLARK HOWELL, JR., Ga.
AYMAR JOHNSON, N. Y.
COL. FREDERIC J. PAXON, Ga.

Assistant Treasurer
A. MACKAY SMITH

Treasurer
DAVE HENNEN MORRIS

GENERAL COMMITTEE

FRANK S. CLARK, Ind.
STUART P. DOBBS, Utah
J. FLOERSHEIM, N. Mex.
J. T. FOWLER, Kan.
ROBERT E. GOULD, N. H.
EARL M. KOUNS, Colo.
R. L. LANFORD, Ark.
E. MCDONALD, Iowa.
R. C. MILLER, Neb.
EWING Y. MITCHELL, Mo.
JOHN B. TANSIL, Mont.
JAMES D. WHELAN, Idaho
MARSH WISEHEART, Ill.

June 18, 1932

Mr. William MacDonald,
Keyser, W. Va.

Dear Sir:

During the Convention the Roosevelt Business and Professional League will have Chicago headquarters at the Congress Hotel, opening June 25th. We hope very much that we may have the pleasure of seeing you there from time to time.

We of course are looking forward to the nomination of Governor Roosevelt, and we would appreciate very much the opportunity for officials of the League to meet you personally while you are in Chicago so that we may all work the most effectively, following the nomination, for a great victory at the polls in November.

Very sincerely yours,

Jesse Isidor Straus

Yet the convention system was complicated. Delegates, who came from all across the country, might shift their votes to another candidate. Sometimes, candidates who were not in the lead gained strength after each convention vote (or ballot), while those who had the majority lost delegates as blocks of opposition formed and grew. At some conventions, it took many ballots to select a candidate.

It took four ballots and a major shift of votes to send FDR over the top and secure his nomination. FDR sat in Albany, listening to the results over the radio. The next day, he and Eleanor flew to Chicago, where he delivered his acceptance speech. The band in the hall played the bouncy tune "Happy Days Are Here Again." Toward the end of his speech, FDR said:

"I pledge you, I pledge myself, to a New Deal for the American people. Let us all here assembled constitute ourselves prophets of a new order of competence and of courage.

This is more than a political campaign; it is a call to arms. Give me your help, not to win votes alone, but to win in this crusade to restore America to its own people."

For many people, the "New Deal" sounded like the fresh start the country needed. One of the many ideas FDR proposed in his acceptance speech was reforestation of vacant lands, similar to what he had done as governor. Another idea he mentioned was abolishing useless offices and waste within the government to save taxpayer money.

Presidential Campaign of 1932

Though she had eagerly supported him thus far in his political career, FDR's mother was not very enthusiastic about her son being the Democratic nominee for president. She felt the presidency was a very tiring and difficult job.

"WE HAVE ALWAYS KNOWN THAT HEEDLESS SELF-INTEREST WAS BAD MORALS;

WE NOW KNOW THAT IT IS BAD ECONOMICS."

—Franklin D. Roosevelt

BY ROBERT MORGENTHAU,
son of Treasury Secretary Henry Morgenthau

"My father and President Roosevelt were [practically] the only two Democrats in Dutchess County. My father and my mother were both close to the Roosevelts. I remember him well before he ran for governor, and then when he became governor, my father was his conservation commissioner, and so we saw him quite often. He lived in Hyde Park, we lived in East Fishkill, which was actually 23 miles away.

I remember my parents always spent New Year's Eve with the Roosevelts. I was with them on a couple of occasions. At midnight, the president would propose a toast to the United States of America, and my father would propose a toast to the president of the United States.

Because he was immobile to a large extent, he was extremely warm and outgoing. He attracted people to come and talk to him. He had a very warm and open personality. And of course he loved to drive himself around in that car, around on his property in Dutchess County and on the road. My father used to drive with him. I've got pictures of it. They had a routine on Election Day where they always drove around together.

He was ambitious, but he didn't show that at all. One of the things that was different in those days, the president really wrote his own speeches. I mean he had help from Robert Sherwood and so on, but I mean now, when a president gives a speech, one thing you know is that the president didn't write a word of it."

FDR and Henry Morgenthau Jr. in a car during the 1930s.

Nonetheless she continued to support him, and knew he would make a good president.

Many people blamed President Hoover for the Depression. Around the country, people who had lost their jobs and their homes had banded together to live in rickety shacks. These settlements became known as Hoovervilles. Much of the country was angry with Hoover. He had promised prosperity, yet once the Depression hit, he was unable to do much to fix it. Still, the Democrats could take nothing for granted. Republicans had been in the White House for 12 years in a row—first Harding, then Coolidge, then Hoover. The presidential campaign had to be taken seriously.

Some so-called progressive Republicans around the country also supported FDR for president. One Republican was quoted about his decision to support FDR as being his "highest political duty" in order to "rid both the party and the nation of Hooverism." Some of these progressives were ironically the same Republicans who had campaigned for the "Bull Moose" Teddy Roosevelt in 1912. One potential problem was that most of the progressive Republicans in the western states were "dries"; that is, they supported the constitutional amendment that had banned the sale of alcoholic beverages. FDR wanted to repeal Prohibition (a move supported by the "wets").

During fall 1932, Franklin Roosevelt rode around the country on a train called the "Roosevelt Special." He made many appearances and gave many speeches, yet nobody knew the true extent of his paralysis. Through his use of heavy leg braces, which helped keep his legs from buckling under him, he was able to stand. With the use of a cane in one hand and holding on to another person with his other hand, FDR was able to give the appearance that he was walking. He also learned to use his upper body strength to sway his shoulders to help give the illusion that he was

Movies: The Great Escape

The movie industry blossomed during the Depression in the 1930s. Millions of Americans went to the movies every week as a means of escaping the harsh realities of their own lives. For 12 cents or less, kids could watch a double feature (two movies) and a newsreel (a few minutes of the most recent news), and sometimes short cartoons like Mickey Mouse.

Musicals and comedies were very popular and featured the top singing and dancing stars of the day in movies featuring elaborate sets and costumes as well as vaudeville comedy stars like Marx Brothers.

Other popular film genres of the 1930s included westerns, gangster films, and detective movies—all in black and white until color was introduced in 1939 in two major blockbusters, *The Wizard of Oz* and *Gone with the Wind*.

walking normally. In reality, FDR was moving, but it was a painful and slow process that was not at all meant for long distances.

When he got to a place where he had to stand to make a speech or pose for the cameras, he most often leaned against a podium or railing, or some other piece of furniture. His sheer determination and energy made it almost seem as if nothing was wrong with him. In his travels across the country, he really got to know the troubles Americans faced, and he listened to their fears and worries. They saw a man who had seemingly overcome his polio.

On Election Day, November 8, 1932, FDR sent a telegram to his running mate, John Nance Garner of Texas. "Best of luck to my good old teammate. Everything points to a victory for us," he wrote. The victory was decisive. FDR had 472 electoral votes to Hoover's 59. The popular vote was 27.8 million to 15.7 million. At 9:30 P.M., Hoover sent a telegram conceding defeat. His carefully worded message began: "I congratulate you on the opportunity that has come to you to be of service to

Art Deco

The late 1920s and 1930s featured a distinct design style known as Art Deco. This style, seen in architecture, jewelry, furniture, product design, and advertising, was the most modern look of the times. Art Deco's main features are curved edges accented by parallel stepped grooves or lines. The most famous Art Deco building is the Chrysler Building (completed 1930) in New York City. The Empire State Building (completed 1932) is another example of Art Deco architecture. Miami, Florida, may have the best examples of Deco architecture in the country.

A 1930s Art Deco radio station.

the country." It was official. Franklin Delano Roosevelt would be the 32nd president of the United States.

A destitute family in a California migrant workers camp, 1936.

4 THE NATION ASKS FOR ACTION

While Franklin Roosevelt was closing out his second term as governor of New York, the nation's economy was in disarray. The Great Depression had entered its fourth year, and the American people were clearly suffering. Poverty was widespread in city and country, from the East Coast to the West Coast. By this time nearly half the banks in the country had failed. About one-third of the population relied on food handouts. More than 15 million people were unemployed. Many people lost their homes because they could not afford to pay their mortgages.

President-Elect

Even before the dust from his election victory had settled, FDR began to plan what he would do once he took office. He was already receiv-ing lots of advice and requests for political favors. One telegram he received in January 1933 told of the difficult economic situation in Washington State: "Conditions in agricultural district east of Cascades in Washington very serious; lumbering and fishing interests on west side in similar condition, resulting in many banks being in frozen condition."

One of the many tasks FDR faced in the first months of 1933 was fitting his friends and supporters into roles in his cabinet and elsewhere in his administration. FDR rewarded loyalty. He offered his 1920 running mate, James Cox, the position of American ambassador to Germany, but Cox turned down the offer, preferring to stay in the newspaper business.

Meanwhile, the economic situation was getting worse. At the end of February 1933, just before FDR was to be inaugurated, a new contagion of fear swept the country, and bank customers began to line up to withdraw their money—cash that the banks had invested in many places. Some of the invested money had been lost during the Depression. The banks simply did not have enough money on hand to satisfy all the customers who wanted cash. FDR itched to take action, but he had to wait until Hoover was out and he was in.

The very day of President-elect Roosevelt's inauguration, March 4, nearly all the banks in the country suspended business. As he awoke that day, the new president understood that he had to take action immediately.

The Banking Crisis and the New Deal

The day before his inauguration, FDR, Eleanor, their son James, and James's wife, Betsey, paid a customary visit to the outgoing president, Herbert Hoover. What was supposed to be a social event seemed to be more than that. When President Hoover entered the White House Green Room, where the Roosevelts waited, he was accompanied by his treasury secretary. What is he doing here, FDR wondered? Hoover wanted FDR to agree to a joint approach to the banking crisis. FDR made it

A ticket to FDR's first inauguration.

INAUGURATION OF THE PRESIDENT AND VICE PRESIDENT OF THE UNITED STATES
WASHINGTON, D.C.   MARCH 4, 1933
Admit One — ★ — $2.00 Tax Exempt
Sec. A   Row 10   Seat 15
Pennsylvania Avenue STAND C

clear he was not there to talk about economic strategy; he did not have any advisors with him in any event. Besides, he had no interest in having his name connected to Hoover's economic policy.

Hoover was not pleased. When it was time to go, FDR tried to be polite and told Hoover that it might take him a while to exit the room because of his handicap, and that he didn't have to wait. Hoover dismissed him coldly, saying, "Mr. Roosevelt, after you have been president for a while, you will learn that the president waits for no one." With that, Hoover left the room.

On the morning of his inauguration in Washington, D.C., FDR attended church, where his old Groton headmaster and friend, Endicott Peabody, led the services. As was tradition, Roosevelt and outgoing president Herbert Hoover sat together as they were driven to the inauguration. It was painfully awkward, especially after the previous day's incident. Though FDR tried to make polite conversion with his opponent, Hoover simply wasn't interested. But FDR had much bigger things to deal with than Hoover. When FDR got to the podium, he saw a crowd of 100,000 people watching him. It was a proud moment for him. As he took the oath of office, he placed his hand on the old Roosevelt family Bible, the same one he had used during his

inaugurations as governor in 1929 and 1931. In his inauguration address, FDR said:

FDR and Herbert Hoover ride to FDR's inauguration, March 1933.

"This is preeminently the time to speak the truth, the whole truth, frankly and boldly. Nor need we shrink from honestly facing conditions in our country today. This great

Nation will endure as it has endured, will revive and will prosper. So, first of all, let me assert my firm belief that the only thing we have to fear is fear itself—nameless, unreasoning, unjustified terror which paralyzes needed efforts to convert retreat into advance. In every dark hour of our national life a leadership of frankness and vigor has met with that understanding and support of the people themselves which is essential to victory. I am convinced that you will again give that support to leadership in these critical days."

Roosevelt wanted to prevent panic from taking over America. In his speech, he also explained that he wanted America to be a "good neighbor" to other countries. At the same time, he told Americans (who were tuning in to him on millions of radios across the country) that international trade relations were secondary to the national economy. He promised to do what he could to protect the homeowner from foreclosure.

There was no time for Franklin to enjoy his new office. He was thrust into the worst economic crisis any president ever faced at his first inauguration. Roosevelt immediately declared an extended national bank holiday and developed a plan to get the banking system reorganized and back on its feet. But President Roosevelt did not stop there.

The coming weeks and months brought a whirlwind of activity in the administration. FDR realized that the federal government would have to expand and get involved in the lives of average Americans to a greater extent than before. A collection of new agencies would have to be created to deal with each of the many problems that faced Americans. The first three months of FDR's presidency were known as the Hundred Days, a time

FDR's inauguration ceremony, March 4, 1933.

when many new laws were enacted to help America recover from the Depression.

On March 5, 1933, FDR sat down to meet with his newly assembled cabinet. He had only appointed people in whom he had the highest confidence. As secretary of agriculture, he named Henry A. Wallace, an agricultural scientist from Iowa. As secretary of labor, he appointed Frances Perkins, the first woman ever to serve a president in a cabinet-level position. He had known her for years, from her labor work in the New York State government. The cabinet members discussed their ideas with Roosevelt.

On March 8, FDR held his first White House press conference. From his time as governor, he was already well aware that the press could be quite helpful in spreading his message. Former reporter Louis Howe helped FDR strategize. On March 9, FDR called the newly installed Congress to an emergency session. Also on March 9, Congress passed the Emergency Banking Act, calling for the reopening of those banks that were stable enough to be saved.

FDR made a point to get on the radio and explain the situation to the American people. In his radio speech of Sunday evening, March 12, 1933 (just eight days after he took office), FDR started by explaining how banks work "for the benefit of the average citizen." He told the country in plain language that banks keep only a portion of their total assets on hand, while the rest is tied up in investments. Though he had given radio talks when he was governor of New York, now his audience was nationwide. Though he had a refined, upper-class accent, Roosevelt was capable of talking to the common people without talking down to them. These radio speeches were known as fireside chats for their down-to-earth, personal tone. During his presidency, FDR gave a total of 30 fireside chats.

In the first radio chat of his presidency, FDR told Americans that he wanted to restructure the country's "financial and economic fabric" and laid out in plain language his plan to get the banks reopened. He used flat-out honesty to make a connection with his listeners, telling them, "We had a bad banking situation" and assuring them that the government was not doing anything complex or radical to correct the crisis.

He explained the situation in these words that Sunday:

First of all let me state the simple fact that when you deposit money in a bank the bank does not put the money into a safe deposit vault. It invests your money in many different forms of credit-bonds, commercial paper, mortgages and many other kinds of loans. In

> "IT IS COMMON SENSE TO TAKE A METHOD AND TRY IT. IF IT FAILS, ADMIT IT FRANKLY AND TRY ANOTHER. BUT ABOVE ALL, TRY SOMETHING."
>
> —Franklin D. Roosevelt

Give a Fireside Chat

PRESIDENT ROOSEVELT'S WEEKLY radio "fireside chats," in which he spoke directly to the American people, ranged in length from 15 to 45 minutes. The topics he chose reflected the pressing issues of the day, including the banking crisis, unemployment, and his New Deal programs. Later, during World War II, he discussed the progress of the war and national security and defense. He used plain language to explain his actions and plans and to reassure the American people. In this activity, you will create and deliver a short "fireside chat" of your own, for today's audience.

YOU'LL NEED
★ Notebook of lined paper
★ Pen or pencil
★ Computer with Internet access
★ Newspapers
★ Library
★ Audience of friends, classmates, or family members

Imagine that you are the president today. Write a three- to five-minute "fireside chat" about the current situation in the country.

Examples of topics include education, unemployment, environmental issues, armed conflict with other countries, and terrorism, to name a few. Use the Internet, newspapers, and books at the library to research your topic so you can present accurate facts to the public. Now, as president, what are your plans to address the situation? Present the problem and then your solution. You will want to be honest and straightforward.

See page 71 for an excerpt from a fireside chat FDR gave on May 7, 1933. See if you get a feel for his style and why he was successful.

After you've written your speech; practice reading it out loud. When you are ready to deliver your speech, gather a small audience of friends and family and see how well it goes over.

other words, the bank puts your money to work to keep the wheels of industry and of agriculture turning around. A comparatively small part of the money you put into the bank is kept in currency—an amount which in normal times is wholly sufficient to cover the cash needs of the average citizen. In other words the total amount of all the currency in the country is only a small fraction of the total deposits in all of the banks.

What, then, happened during the last few days of February and the first few days of March? Because of undermined confidence on the part of the public, there was a general rush by a large portion of our population to turn bank deposits into currency or gold. A rush so great that the soundest banks could not get enough currency to meet the demand. The reason for this was that on the spur of the moment it was, of course, impossible to sell perfectly sound assets of a bank and convert them into cash except at panic prices far below their real value.**"**

While he was optimistic about jump-starting the nation's banks, Roosevelt was careful not to promise that everything would be OK for everyone. After all, though he was an optimist, he was also a realist. He acknowledged that some banks might never reopen, and that it was likely that some people would in fact lose their money. Roosevelt was a strong believer in knowledge as a weapon and felt that ignorance was a menace. He knew that the most dangerous enemy of the American people was fear and panic. In a sense, it was worse for people to fear the unknown about the banking crisis, rather than know and accept what might be a bittersweet truth. He felt that confidence was what needed to be restored, confidence that the government was doing everything it could, and confidence in the American banking system.

In closing, he said: "You people must have faith; you must not be stampeded by rumors or guesses. Let us unite in banishing fear. We have provided the machinery to restore our financial system; it is up to you to support and make it work. It is your problem no less than it is mine. Together we cannot fail."

FDR understood that the next step was to take the United States off the "gold standard." This meant that paper and coin money could no longer be exchanged at the bank for gold. In fact, FDR wanted Americans who had more than a couple of gold coins to turn in their gold. The hoarding of gold was not good for the economy. Taking excess gold out of private hands gave a boost to the monetary system by placing more trust into paper money. That is why on March 6, 1933, FDR had issued a proclamation that made it illegal for people to hoard gold.

The measures that FDR took to resolve the banking crisis were just a small part of the "New Deal" he had promised. As the weeks and months passed, he and his cabinet busily came up with new programs to address problems in nearly every sector of the economy. Each one had a catchy name and was known by an abbreviation (or acronym). Each one also had its opponents. Among the agencies created were the Tennessee Valley Authority (TVA), the Agricultural Adjustment Act (AAA), the National Recovery Administration (NRA), the Works Progress Administration (WPA), and the Civilian Conservation Corps (CCC).

The TVA was created in order to use government-owned land along the Tennessee River to provide water-generated power for many thousands of people in seven states along the river. This created many jobs and helped

Franklin and Eleanor Roosevelt in 1933.

"THE ONLY THING WE HAVE TO FEAR IS FEAR ITSELF."

—Franklin D. Roosevelt

some of the poorer people in the country get electricity. Still, power companies opposed the TVA because it took away their business. They felt the government had no right to get into the business of providing power. The TVA was also concerned with creating better drainage for storm-water runoff and preventing soil erosion. Runoff is rainwater that falls in one place and then flows and drains elsewhere (either into the ground, into standing water, or into a sewer). Through their efforts, the TVA helped make thousands of acres of land usable again.

The AAA was an innovative idea, developed by Secretary of Agriculture Henry Wallace, who understood the economics of farming. He understood that farmers wanted to get the most money for their crops, so they tried to grow as much as possible. That way they could have a large amount to sell to food processors and manufacturers. Though this would seem to be the right approach, it backfired. Too many farmers were growing too much. Instead of prices going up, they went down because there was too much corn and wheat available. So farmers were growing more but actually getting less money.

What Wallace proposed was to pay farmers to reduce their output of seven crops—wheat, corn, cotton, rice, tobacco, peanuts, and milk. In other words, he wanted to pay farmers *not* to grow crops. In addition, Wallace wanted to impose a tax on the food processors in order to pay for the incentives given to the farmers. The consumer then felt the pinch with an increase in processed food prices that the processors passed along to make up for the tax. Not only that, but some surplus crops were actually destroyed. Millions of acres of cotton and millions of pigs were destroyed without ever going to market. FDR agreed with the proposed plan.

The measure passed in Congress, but many people thought these ideas were insane. How could anyone want to reduce production? Then again, most people did not understand

Young Republicans Didn't Clap

BY VICTORIA WIRTH,
daughter of attorney Arthur A. Henning

"My father, who was admitted to the New York Bar Association with FDR [in 1907], was active in the Bronx Democratic Party, but my mother was a staunch Republican. We girls [three sisters] also were Republican, and we were the only ones in our elementary school who were! Everyone seemed to love FDR, and when he was shown on the Movietone News everyone clapped—except us, of course."

the economics of supply and demand. Within about a year, crop prices were up more than 40 percent. As FDR told Americans in July 1933, "Without our help the farmers cannot get together and cut production, and the Farm Bill gives them a method of bringing their production down to a reasonable level and of obtaining reasonable prices for their crops."

Not everyone agreed with the Farm Bill. John Sam Johnson of Huntersville, North Carolina, said in an interview in 1939:

"All the land you see around here belongs to me. I could make a lot of stuff on it if it wasn't for that fellow Roosevelt, sitting up in the White House, dictating to the farmers—I wasn't allowed to plant but four acres in cotton this time; it's going to make about six bales—maybe I'm just ignorant and don't know what I'm talking about, but I do know one thing—I didn't help put this president in office and I sure will do all I can to get him out."

The National Recovery Administration was an unpopular agency that dealt with regulating business to try to stimulate the economy and ensure fairness. It wound up challenged in the Supreme Court (see page 81).

Another large-scale program of the New Deal was the Civilian Conservation Corps (CCC). Since his boyhood, FDR loved nature and enjoyed planting trees; it is estimated that he planted tens of thousands of trees in his lifetime. As governor he had pushed for reforestation in New York State. It bothered FDR that great old trees all across the country were being chopped down by the millions and not replaced. He proposed the reforestation idea and left it to Labor Secretary Frances Perkins and others to work out the details of how it would be accomplished. The goal was to employ up to 250,000 workers at wages of one dollar per day (plus room and board). In addition to reforestation, they would be doing

CCC workers in Idaho transplant beavers to a location where they will help conserve the water supply, 1938.

→ Beautify Your School

MOST NEW DEAL programs not only put people to work but also put them into meaningful public service jobs. FDR wanted to get America back on track by putting idle people to work on important missions that would make a difference in quality of life. Among other things, the WPA and CCC workers cleaned up neighborhoods, planted trees to prevent erosion and break up windstorms, and put artists to work painting inspiring murals in public buildings. In this activity you will perform a public service for your neighborhood by helping plant flowers and/or trees on your school property.

Adult supervision required

YOU'LL NEED
* ★ Fabric work gloves or thick rubber gloves
* ★ Notebook and pencil
* ★ Classmates
* ★ Small shovels
* ★ Access to a watering hose and connection
* ★ Annual or perennial flowering plants and/or shrubs/trees

Note: Check with the principal or superintendent before you begin any plans.

Figure out where on your school property flowers or shrubs/small trees could improve the appearance of the property and not interfere with any school activities. Make a map of the school property and decide what to plant where. With just a few dollars' donation from each student, the class can buy a nice selection of plants. Note that different plants need differing amounts of sunshine. Plants such as impatiens can do well in shade.

Make sure you loosen the dirt in the planting area before you dig holes for the plants. Make your holes about twice as wide as the plant's root ball, then place the plant in the hole and refill. Follow planting directions for spacing of plants. Water thoroughly after planting, and make sure you water at least twice a week when rain is not in the forecast. Remember that most plants will grow and spread out over time, filling in the space between them.

other outdoor tasks including road repairs, and landscaping to prevent floods and soil erosion. Under the CCC, land was also purchased by the government to enlarge some of the existing national forests. Over the years of its existence, leading up to World War II, CCC workers planted about 200 million trees.

FDR used every means possible to get out the message about the New Deal. His postmaster general, James Farley, worked with him. The National Recovery Administration was featured on a three-cent stamp released on August 15, 1933. The stamp showed a farmer, a blacksmith, a businessman, and a young woman standing together. At the bottom it said, "In a common determination." Farley sent FDR the finished stamp, and the president wrote back immediately to congratulate Farley. He said "it is a grand stamp, gotten out in record time, and will do worlds of good."

Another New Deal agency, the Federal Emergency Relief Administration (FERA), allotted hundreds of millions of dollars for solving the unemployment problem. One of the most important parts of FERA was the Emergency Education Program (EEP), which provided education for adults to reduce illiteracy and therefore help them get better jobs.

Out of FERA grew other important programs, including the Civil Works Administration and the Works Progress Administration

(WPA). During the 1930s, the WPA helped millions of unemployed people. The beauty of this program was that it also included people who were not blue-collar laborers. It included artists, writers, and other creative people. Artists were employed in producing large-scale murals and other art that could be enjoyed by the public, in government buildings and in outdoor plazas. In fact, the Federal Art Project and the earlier Public Works of Art Project employed thousands of artists.

Writers contributed through the Federal Writers' Project. The Writers' Project employed thousands of writers, who produced guides to each of the states and conducted and transcribed interviews with common people about their lives and times. These works were a lasting gift of the New Deal, and a symbol of the idea of the WPA—finding ways to give relief to the unemployed while getting something in return.

The Home Owners' Loan Act (HOLA) provided more than $2 billion for the refinancing of mortgages. This was needed relief because people who had little or no money were still required to pay their old mortgage amounts on properties whose values had declined. Unable to pay after several years of the Depression, they now faced the loss of their homes. The Act provided new mortgages for one million such people nationwide.

At the time they were introduced, not everyone was pleased with these programs. FDR's Republican opponents thought his New Deal was quite similar to the kind of program that the communists would favor. They thought that FDR was giving the government too much control and responsibility over people's lives.

Because there seemed to be some misunderstanding of the inner workings and reasoning behind New Deal programs, FDR sometimes had to defend his policies. In May 1933, he tried to reassure Americans that the New Deal was in the best interests of the country, and was already working:

"First, we are giving opportunity of employment to one-quarter of a million of the unemployed, especially the young men who have dependents, to go into the forestry and flood prevention work. This is a big task because it means feeding, clothing, and caring for nearly twice as many men as we have in the regular army itself. In creating this civilian conservation corps we are killing two birds with one stone."

At the end of his speech, he said: "Every ounce of strength and every resource at our command we have devoted to the end of justifying your confidence. We are encouraged to believe that a wise and sensible beginning

"I THINK WE CONSIDER TOO MUCH THE GOOD LUCK OF THE EARLY BIRD AND NOT ENOUGH THE BAD LUCK OF THE EARLY WORM."
—Franklin D. Roosevelt

A National Recovery Administration (NRA) sticker.

has been made. In the present spirit of mutual confidence and mutual encouragement we go forward."

In July 1933, FDR was on the radio again, speaking to the general public. People across the country sat in their living rooms, ears glued to their radio sets, as the president told them:

"When Andrew Jackson, 'Old Hickory,' died, someone asked, 'Will he go to Heaven?' and the answer was, 'He will if he wants to.' If I am asked whether the American people will pull themselves out of this depression, I answer, 'They will if they want to' . . . I have no faith in 'cure-alls' but I believe that we can greatly influence economic forces. I have no sympathy with the professional economists who insist that things must run their course. . . ."

The road to economic recovery was rocky. In early July 1933, there were signs of resurgence, but by September things looked bleak again. As 1933 turned into 1934, the New Deal continued to expand. There were definite successes that FDR could point to, such as the increase in prices for crops, and an increase in employment. At the same time, the New Deal was so large and complicated, there was no way for FDR to be involved in every minute aspect of all the programs. He relied heavily upon his cabinet and the people he had appointed to head the various agencies to ensure everything ran smoothly.

A biography of FDR published in mid-1934 warned that there were still 10 million people unemployed throughout the country, but called the New Deal a good beginning, saying it had restored faith in democracy.

The National Youth Administration was created in 1935 in order to create part-time jobs for high school, college, and graduate students. These young people worked on highways and other public works projects around the country.

In his speeches to the American public, FDR tried to make them feel like they had some say in the recovery process. In 1935, FDR told Americans, "I, therefore, hope you will watch the work in every corner of this Nation. Feel free to criticize. Tell me of instances where work can be done better, or where improper practices prevail."

The Social Security Act

FDR was pleased with the New Deal programs that had been introduced. He felt they were working. Still, he felt there was more to do for the average American. Providing jobs through the CCC and the WPA was a good

⇒ Be a WPA Historian

THE WORKS PROGRESS Administration (WPA) created numerous opportunities for writers and artists to work and at the same time provide a service to their community. The Writers' Project, part of the WPA, sponsored the study of American folklore—the unique customs and lifestyles of Americans in different parts of the country. It was at the time the most ambitious oral history program ever conducted. Now, historians collect oral histories of Holocaust survivors, World War II veterans, and others.

Each state had its own program under the Writers' Project. The Virginia Writers' Project (VWP), for example, studied local folklore in all the different regions of the state. They conducted over 1,500 interviews, including 300 with former slaves. In many cases, Writers' Project workers were likely to take oral histories of older members of certain communities because they represented a generation whose stories would die with them unless recorded. In one case, a 91-year-old man named Lycurgus Drumheller was interviewed in 1939 about his life and the songs, dances, and games he remembered from his childhood in the 1850s, including Chicka-

my Crany Crow, Killyme Kranky, and London Bridge. In this activity you will record the childhood memories of an adult you know.

YOU'LL NEED
★ Notebook
★ Tape recorder (optional)
★ Pen
★ Computer (optional)

Make a list of people you would like to interview. Family members may be a good place to

Two WPA posters

start—even older siblings or cousins. The people you interview can tell you what games they played as kids, what hobbies they had, what chores or jobs they had, what television or radio shows were popular, and where they liked to hang out as kids. Remember, some subjects may think they have nothing interesting to say. As an interviewer, your job is to be interested and keep them talking. As the members of the WPA Writers' Project believed, everyone has something interesting to say about how and where they live or about their childhood.

Record your subjects' memories as best you can. Note the year they were born and where they lived. Research (use the Internet, an almanac, or an encyclopedia) and write down the current population of the town. If you have a tape recorder, you can record the interview, then later transcribe (write or type out) exactly what was said. If not, you can take notes during the interview and then summarize what your subject told you in essay format. When you are done, you can present your subject with a copy of the transcribed interview or essay.

➡ Paint a WPA-Style Mural

ONE OF FDR'S New Deal programs, the WPA, employed many artists painting murals—large-scale paintings on the walls and ceilings of public buildings. You may have seen a mural in your neighborhood or perhaps even in your school. WPA murals usually featured scenes of people hard at work, or captured moments in the country's history. They were meant to inspire people

A 1934 mural titled *The New Deal* and featuring FDR with a symbolic helping hand on a worker's shoulder.

and give them hope during hard times. In this activity, you will create a mural of your own.

YOU'LL NEED
★ 5 friends
★ Several sheets of white, 8½ × 11-inch paper
★ Scissors
★ Ruler
★ Pencil
★ 6 sheets of 30 × 40-inch foam board
★ Tempera paints (green, blue, yellow, red, white, black)
★ 6 or more paintbrushes (in a variety of thicknesses)
★ 6 or more plastic bowls
★ Double-sided tape or push pins

The first thing a mural painter needs to do is develop a plan for the mural. Take a sheet of white paper and cut it down to 5 × 10 inches. This is the shape your mural will be. Using the ruler and pencil, divide the paper into six equal sections (three columns of 3¼ inches and two rows of 2½ inches). Each rectangle represents one of your foam board mural pieces. What kind of scene do you want to depict? A WPA-style mural

would have shown people at work, children happily studying, or your city or neighborhood looking vibrant. Work with others to develop an idea and then sketch it out on the paper. Draw rough outlines for people, trees, buildings, etc., to show their position and relative size. When you have it right, carefully transfer the pencil outline to the foam boards by laying them on the floor three across and two deep.

Pour each tempera paint color into its own bowl. You may want to mix your own colors as well and put them into bowls also. Next, assign the painting duties. You could have one person paint all the trees and shrubs and another person paint all the people. Or one person could paint the rough images of people while another could then fill in the details. Another person could paint all the buildings, or the sky. The important thing is to work together so that when all the panels are put together they have the same overall style.

When you have finished all six panels and the paint is dry, your six-piece mural is ready to assemble and hang. Work with an adult to figure out how and where to hang the panels. Strong double-sided tape or long pushpins might be useful.

start, but not everyone would be able to find a job right away. For some of the people who had lost their jobs, it might take months to find another, and FDR felt they needed some assistance during those unemployed months.

In addition to this dilemma, another issue troubled FDR. He noted that the U.S. government did virtually nothing to take care of its elderly. People who had worked all their lives, 40 or even 50 years, were now struggling to live out their retirement. As modern medicine helped people live longer, these same people were living in poverty as their savings dried up. FDR felt that a government-sponsored pension was the answer.

FDR had had the seeds of these ideas since before his inauguration in 1933. He watched with disappointment as an unemployment insurance bill drafted by two senators, called the Wagner-Lewis bill, stalled in Congress in 1934. Something more had to be done. FDR appointed a cabinet-level committee on economic security that included Secretary of Labor Frances Perkins, Secretary of the Treasury Henry Morgenthau, and Secretary of Agriculture Henry Wallace, among others.

The Economic Security Bill drafted by the Roosevelt administration was sent to Congress in January 1935. Renamed the Social Security Act in March, it called for two key things—unemployment insurance for those who were out of work, and social security for retired workers who were over the age of 65.

The social security system provided a minimum monthly benefit of $10 (up to a maximum of $85 per month). The amount depended on how many years of employment a person had contributed and what his or her salary was. The system also provided a special one-time payment called a "death benefit" to a surviving spouse, and benefits to those who were injured or became sick and could not work.

The difference between these ideas and the rest of the New Deal was that members of FDR's cabinet recommended that this system be permanent, to provide security to all, regardless of whether the economy was failing, or whether some people were better off than others. It did not matter if unemployed people had $3 or $30,000 in the bank; they were entitled to assistance.

FDR was very excited about the proposed system of social insurance. He wanted it to be simple and clear, and for Americans to know that they would be covered by this system from the time they were born through their old age. All citizens would have a unique social security number that would allow the government to identify and track them through their lives, and to easily provide assistance when it was needed and social security benefits when they turned 65. To help fund this, the Social

A drawing of FDR by a New York teenager, 1934.

Security Act also called for employers to pay a tax on their employees.

The president especially insisted upon making sure that unemployment insurance was established. Through the Social Security Act, millions of federal dollars were set aside to give to states so they could administer unemployment insurance programs. FDR even wanted to include some kind of universal health insurance in the legislation, but the odds seemed too great against that happening.

Though it would help millions of Americans, the Social Security Act was a risky policy at the time. It meant more government involvement in individuals' lives. Some FDR enemies called this and other New Deal legislation socialism.

Nonetheless, the bill passed without any trouble in the House of Representatives by a vote of 372–33, and then in the Senate in June 1935 by a vote of 77–6. In a letter dated April 21, 1935, FDR wrote, "After all the howls and squawks the Social Security Bill passed the House with only thirty-three votes against it." Once signed by the president, it became official.

In the many decades since Social Security was implemented, tens of millions of Americans have been able to live more comfortably through retirement knowing that every month, a government check would be waiting for them in their mailbox. Though some even today question the soundness of the system, it remains one of President Roosevelt's greatest accomplishments.

Memories of FDR

BY GEORGE MCGOVERN,
senator and 1972 Democratic presidential candidate

"He was the greatest president of the 20th century without question. He led us out of the Depression, and he led us to victory in World War II, two crowning achievements. Of course, he was elected to four terms. I think the New Deal was the great charter of progress on the social and economic fronts. Frankly, most of the New Deal is still in operation, including Social Security. My father and mother lived and died as conservative Republicans, but I never heard them say a critical word about Franklin Roosevelt. His dedication to rank and file Americans was always what inspired me. Putting people back to work, providing social security for those out of work, for the injured and disabled. It was a comprehensive social security for tens of millions of Americans who were otherwise unable to provide for themselves, and it meant a lot during the 1930s.

One of the things that inspired me growing up in South Dakota was the planting of shelter belts, the planting of trees across the state to break up wind and dust storms. It would be the middle of the day, and it would get as dark as night during one of those storms. The shelter belts broke them up. That was the first thing I appreciated from the New Deal."

Trouble Brewing in Europe

Average Americans in 1933 and 1934 were concerned with practically nothing else but the Depression. It was a struggle to keep food on the table, let alone worry about what was going on elsewhere in the world. But, in fact, much was going on. In Europe, what had seemed like cautious stability that dominated since the end of World War I was taking a turn for the worse during the 1930s.

The 1932 elections in Germany brought Adolf Hitler and his National Socialist German Worker's Party (Nazi Party for short) to power, and Hitler became chancellor of Germany. Germany's economic depression after World War I had led to the surge in nationalism that Hitler rode into power. In October 1933, Hitler announced that Germany was withdrawing from the League of Nations. By 1934, the Nazis had taken complete control over Germany and were rearming. At one point early in FDR's presidency, Hitler said he admired FDR for his ability to get what he wanted, whether Congress wanted it or not.

In Italy, Benito Mussolini had seized control of the government during the 1920s, and there were now disturbing signs that he wanted to invade Africa.

The world of 1933 seemed much more dangerous than it had just a few years earlier. On

A dust storm on the Great Plains in 1936.

May 16, 1933, President Roosevelt sent a letter to 53 world leaders telling them that the nations of the world must eliminate offensive weapons and enter into a pact of non-aggression. Many of these world leaders wrote back to thank the president for his kind letter and to express their own hopes for peace.

By the summer of 1935, Mussolini was preparing to invade Ethiopia. Still, FDR did not yet think Mussolini was as much a threat as Hitler, and tried to maintain communication with him. He was sticking to the "good neighbor policy" that he had laid out in his inaugural address in 1933.

In 1935, Congress passed the Neutrality Act, which said the United States officially wanted to remain neutral. This was done even

> "IF CIVILIZATION IS TO SURVIVE, WE MUST CULTIVATE THE SCIENCE OF HUMAN RELATIONSHIPS— THE ABILITY OF ALL PEOPLES, OF ALL KINDS, TO LIVE TOGETHER, IN THE SAME WORLD AT PEACE."
>
> —Franklin D. Roosevelt

as Hitler was rearming Germany. After the costly World War I, Americans simply had no interest in getting tangled in foreign affairs. That had been a key reason why Cox and Roosevelt lost in 1920. Not only that, making any real effort to get involved in world politics would cost money, something most people felt would be better spent fixing the problems at home. There was a very complicated network of relationships among the Communists, Fascists, and other political parties of different countries. For the moment, America simply preferred to watch from a distance.

FDR watched the international news and did not like what he saw. He also watched warily as some members of Congress tried to find ways to keep the United States out of war no matter what. FDR did not approve of these "wild-eyed measures" and wrote about these

representatives and senators in a letter dated September 1935: "They imagine that if the civilization of Europe is about to destroy itself through internal strife, it might just as well go ahead and do it and that the United States can stand idly by."

Unlike many in the federal government who wanted to look the other way, FDR preferred to take a wait-and-see approach. From his speeches, it is clear that FDR was torn between wanting to avoid war and wanting to help. By 1936, he admitted that he was more concerned about the world situation as a whole than he was about the domestic situation, yet in the same speech he also said: "I hate war. I have passed unnumbered hours, I shall pass unnumbered hours, thinking and planning how war may be kept from this nation. I wish I could keep war from all nations; but that is beyond my power."

The Fascists

Fascism is a political philosophy or movement that values nation and often race above the individual. The Fascists believed in absolute power for a dictator, expansion of their countries, and suppression of opposition by force, even at the expense of lives. Fascist governments controlled every aspect of people's lives. Adolf Hitler and Benito Mussolini were both Fascists who planned to create empires and ignore the world's opinion of their plans.

Reelection Campaign

By the time 1935 ended and 1936 began, it was nearly time to campaign again. So much had been accomplished in three years, but there was still so much more to do. The Republicans were planning their strategy to defeat FDR. They had a little help from FDR's former friend Alfred Smith, who spoke out against the New Deal at an American Liberty League (a group formed to gather support for defeating FDR) dinner in January 1936. But, on the other hand, FDR got help from some progressive Republicans who were on his side, including Senator Hiram Johnson of California.

Though some felt FDR would have no trouble in November, FDR himself felt only cautiously optimistic. In June 1936, he said, "it is fairly clear that the Republicans will have an enormous campaign chest and will seek every possible advantage, fair and unfair."

FDR was very involved in the day-to-day operations of the campaign, deciding policy on speeches and pamphlets. He was easily nominated at the Democratic National Convention in Philadelphia. He understood that the New Deal had its enemies, and that he would be criticized during the campaign. He tried to let Americans know he was only acting with the best of intentions. Upon being nominated, he said:

"Presidents do make mistakes, but the immortal Dante tells us that divine justice weighs the sins of the cold blooded and the sins of the warm hearted in different scales. . . . Better the occasional faults of a government that lives in a spirit of charity than the consistent omissions of a government frozen in the ice of its own indifference."

Once again, James Farley led FDR's campaign efforts. The president's Republican opponent was Alfred Landon, the governor of Kansas. The Republicans focused on what some Americans were saying about the New Deal—that it was too costly and too invasive. His opponents pointed to the $15,000 that was spent by the federal government every minute on the New Deal. The Republicans were not even convinced FDR's New Deal policies were working so well.

As 1936 progressed, FDR's friend and confidant Louis Howe became very sick. When he died in the winter of 1936, Roosevelt was crushed by the sudden loss. He also referred to the "drag-down-knock-out fight of the campaign." During the last two weeks of the campaign, the Republicans attacked FDR's Social Security bill. Even some ordinary citizens had mixed feelings about FDR's New Deal policies. Claude W. of New York wrote to a friend in Missouri on June 25, 1936:

"Business conditions seem improving right along but I do not think we will ever see all the unemployed back at work, unless we reduce the working hours and week days; there has been too many females that have taken up jobs that should go to men, however Roosevelt is doing a good job and if they will only let him carry out his ideas we will

Campaign buttons, 1936.

A clever Republican campaign giveaway from 1936. The reverse is a mirror.

all at least have social security and there will be no starving to death, however, I am afraid quite a number of people now on relief will get in the habit of not working and will not work if the opportunity offers.*

In his final campaign speech, FDR did not attack anyone. He simply stressed the importance of voting: "Every man and woman who votes tomorrow will have a hand in the making of the United States of the future. To refuse to vote is to say: 'I am not interested in the United States of the future.'"

On Election Day, Franklin Delano Roosevelt was elected by a margin of 27 million to 16 million votes. He won in a landslide, 523

to 8 electoral votes. As James Farley had predicted, FDR won all states except Maine and Vermont. The Democrats also made gains in Congress.

After FDR's victory in November, he wrote a letter to his friend, former Secretary of the Navy Josephus Daniels, saying

Thanks the Lord it was not a close vote or even a gain for Brother Landon over what Herbert Hoover got in 1932. If Landon had got . . . 120 or 130 votes in the electoral college . . . the reactionary element would have used that fact everlastingly during the next two years . . . the campaign, as Jim Farley predicted in June, was a dirty one, but I am thankful the dirt was 99 per cent on the Republican side.

FDR received a letter of congratulations from the Italian dictator Benito Mussolini. He told the president that he hoped "our relations, now re-established, may not undergo any further interruptions."

Eleanor's "My Day" Newspaper Column

As her husband's career advanced first in Albany and then in Washington, the shy and

Memories of FDR

BY KITTY CARLISLE HART,
film actress and singer, widow of playwright Moss Hart

"I met Franklin Delano Roosevelt when I sang 'The Star-Spangled Banner' at the 1936 [Democratic National] Convention. I shook his hand, and I was very impressed. I loved him. I thought he was wonderful. I was proud to sing 'The Star-Spangled Banner' at the convention in Philadelphia. [Eleanor] liked my husband very much. We went to Hyde Park for dinner, and she gave Moss a very nice picture engraved [autographed] to him."

awkward Eleanor Roosevelt of old gradually disappeared. By the time FDR took office as president, Eleanor Roosevelt was much more confident. Though at first she was not terribly happy to be first lady, she quickly realized she ought to get used to her role and make the best of it. She was unafraid to offer her advice to the president, and he was happy to hear it.

Eleanor wrote her first book, *It's Up to the Women*, in 1933. It was a book of advice and anecdotes meant to provide inspiration for women. At the very end of 1935, she began to write a column about her life as first lady and about the events of the day. Called "My Day," the column was published in about 60 newspapers across the country. Her cousin Alice Roosevelt Longworth (daughter of Teddy Roosevelt) also happened to write a newspaper column. Though the cousins did not always see eye to eye, they were still family.

Memories of FDR

BY BETHINE CHURCH,
daughter of Chase Addison Clark, governor of Idaho and FDR-appointed judge

"I met President and Eleanor Roosevelt in 1936, when I was 13. I can still see them standing there, covered in dust after a trip in an open touring car through Yellowstone Park. My father, then mayor of Idaho Falls, and other area officials had been invited to meet them in West Yellowstone. Long before the days of tight presidential security, Pop simply took me along. In spite of reports to the contrary, I found Eleanor Roosevelt beautiful, with her blue eyes and blue chiffon scarf tied haphazardly around her hair. She treated me like a grown-up and an equal. The president thanked me for the wonderful day in my park. Naturally I was thrilled, feeling that I alone had made his experience possible. This moment captured my young heart and wedded it forever to politics."

"YOU GAIN STRENGTH, COURAGE, AND CONFIDENCE BY EVERY EXPERIENCE IN WHICH YOU REALLY STOP TO LOOK FEAR IN THE FACE. . . . YOU MUST DO THE THING YOU THINK YOU CANNOT DO."
—Eleanor Roosevelt

Eleanor talked intelligently about politics and helped publicize her husband's New Deal policies. The day after the Supreme Court struck down the Agricultural Adjustment Act (see page 81), Eleanor wrote in her column that she was surprised to find her hus-band in good spirits, going for a swim in the pool. Eleanor was not afraid to criticize FDR's enemies and spoke out for those measures in which she believed.

Eleanor began work on an autobiography in 1936. It covered her life from her birth to 1924. She dedicated the book to the father who "fired" her imagination. In the book, Eleanor told the honest story of her childhood and detailed all the ups and downs of her life. She explained to her readers that her ability to think for herself was something that did not come until she was well into adulthood. The book jacket called the book "frank, humorous, fearless." Between the book and the column, she became even more popular among Americans, and especially among American women, many of whom identified with her.

Passionate about issues of poverty and civil rights, Eleanor gave many speeches and traveled thousands of miles around the country, visiting communities large and small. The bylines of her columns reflected her travels—Tennessee, Alabama, West Virginia, Oklahoma, Washington—no first lady before her had ever been so active and vocal. Eleanor did what the president could not. She could walk, and Franklin could not. She was tireless in her efforts, an ambassador of good will for the Roosevelt presidency.

Memories of FDR and Eleanor

BY ELEANOR SEAGRAVES,
Franklin and Eleanor Roosevelt's first grandchild

"My brother, Curtis ('Buzzy' as he was known in the 1930s, while I was 'Sisty'), and I lived with our mother, Anna, at the White House for a full year [1934] when I was seven, and my brother four, and then off and on through 1944–1945, summers and Christmas holidays. We loved both grandparents (PaPa and Grandmere). They both were busy people, but made brief and warm times for us before school in the mornings, or just before our early bedtimes. Later, as teenagers, we were conscious of living in the White House, but since we'd lived there so often, it was totally familiar and not awesome. It was simply one of our homes. My grandmother impressed upon us that the White House was 'the people's house.' We were accustomed to meeting and seeing people of various races and cultures circulating throughout the family quarters, or with us at mealtimes.

Observing the generous and cheerful attitudes of family and house staff, I could not help but absorb an interested curiosity about the world, combined with the open hospitality that prevailed on the parts of my mother and her parents."

The Supreme Court Fiasco

FDR's opponents did use one ugly incident as ammunition when some of FDR's New Deal programs were challenged in court. Several of these challenges made it all the way to the Supreme Court. It began on May 27, 1935, when the Court declared that Roosevelt's National Industrial Recovery Act went beyond the powers the constitution said the government could have over business, and was therefore unconstitutional. In 1936, the Supreme Court also struck down the Agriculture Adjustment Act as unconstitutional. Though FDR counted on opposition, he did not expect this. He was angry and felt that the Supreme Court was getting too strong and upsetting the balance among the three branches of government.

It struck FDR to find a way to even the balance a bit. At that time, seven of the nine sitting justices had been appointed by Republican presidents. Roosevelt felt that these Republican-appointed justices were less friendly toward his "big government" policies. To try to change the situation on the Court, FDR came up with a proposal to increase the number of justices on the Supreme Court to as many as 14, depending on the ages of the sitting justices. Doing that would mean he would get to appoint the new justices.

He defended his plan in one of his fireside chats in 1937, denying that he had any personal motives: "If by that phrase 'packing the Court' it is charged that I wish to place on the bench spineless puppets who would disregard the law and would decide specific cases as I wished them to be decided, I make this answer: that no president fit for his office would appoint . . . that kind of appointees to the Supreme Court."

The measure did not gain much support, and eventually died a quiet death when the Senate voted against it overwhelmingly on July 22, 1937, by a margin of 70 to 20. Even Democrats voted against the measure. FDR was not pleased, but what he didn't realize at that moment was that during the next six years, he would have the chance to appoint several Supreme Court justices anyway.

The challenges did not stop FDR from creating more New Deal policies. In 1938, he signed the Fair Labor Standards Act (FLSA), which set a 25-cent-per-hour minimum wage and other groundbreaking standards for the workplace.

Filming of a Supreme Court justice at work during the "court-packing" controversy.

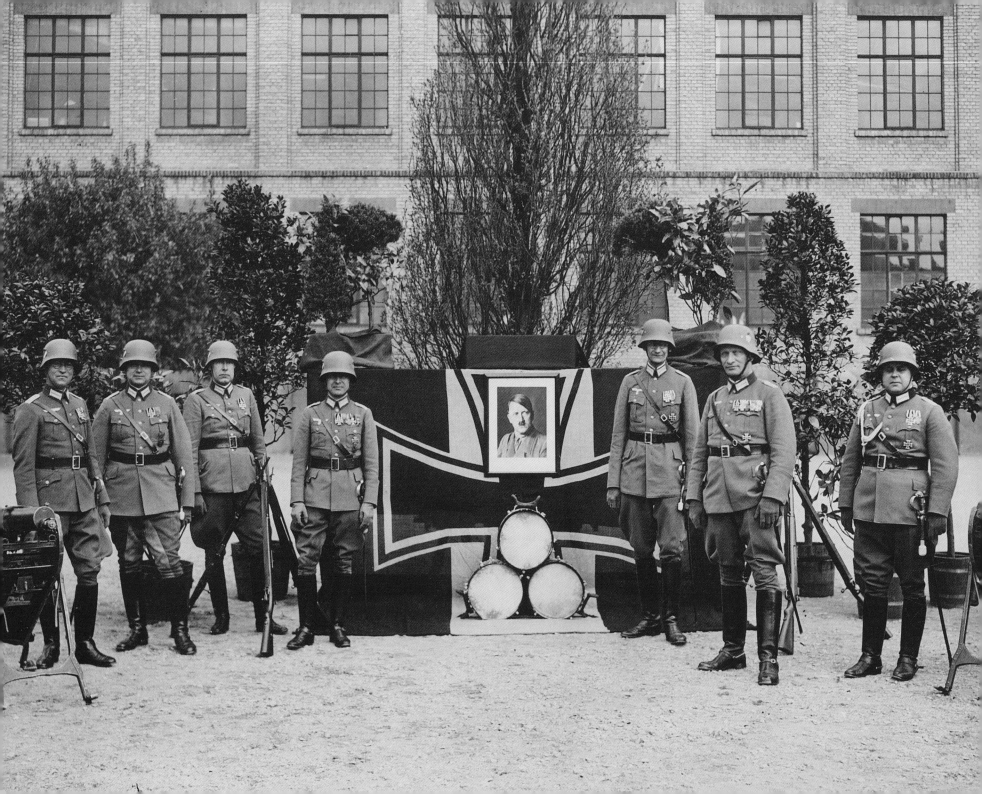

5 DEMOCRACY IN PERIL

Just as the New Deal programs really began to take the edge off the Depression, Americans had something new to worry about. By the spring of 1938, the situation in Europe was indeed grim. There was no more ignoring it. Even those Americans who did not want to think about Hitler worried about him. They still remembered the horrors of the First World War. The events in Europe practically screamed from the American newspaper headlines.

Prelude to War

In March 1938, Germany sent troops to neighboring Austria and took it over. Next, Hitler made plans to annex a German-speaking part of neighboring Czechoslovakia called the Sudetenland. He was ready to do it by force, but the prime minister of England, Neville Chamberlain, wanted to prevent a crisis. In September 1938, FDR composed a letter to the governments of England, France, Czechoslovakia, and Germany asking that a peaceful solution be found. Hitler's reply to FDR was that the World War I peace treaty had not been fair to Germany, and that the League of Nations had not done its job.

When Chamberlain went to Germany and met with Adolf Hitler, he wound up giving in and letting Hitler take Sudetenland. Chamberlain wanted Hitler to stop there, but Hitler was still not satisfied. In March 1939, the German army rolled into the rest of Czechoslovakia.

Even though Americans could not ignore the events in Europe, many people in the country were still dead set against the United States ever becoming involved in a war. But

FDR was a realist. He had already begun to steer the country away from complete isolationism. He delivered a message to Congress in January 1939 that explained how Americans must act with methods that were stronger than words alone, but short of war.

During this time of crisis, FDR relied heavily upon his ambassador to Great Britain, Joseph Kennedy, to keep him updated about the situation and about the general feeling in England about a possible war. Kennedy was convinced that the outlook was bleak for Great Britain, should it enter the war.

Roosevelt's Dilemma

FDR was deeply conflicted. He believed in his heart that the United States must be a member of the world community. At the same time, he knew that such sentiments had helped defeat him in the 1920 election. He knew that even 20 years later, most Americans still desired to stay out of European affairs. FDR had traveled through Europe as a child, and later on his honeymoon, and then again during World War I as assistant secretary of the navy. More than the average American, he understood the nations of Europe.

Roosevelt did not wish to give in to Hitler, but he also did not want to take any forceful action just yet. In April 1939, FDR wrote a

Hitler's photo is displayed at a Nazi ceremony in the mid-1930s.

long letter to Hitler (a similar letter was sent to Mussolini). His tone in the letter was polite, but he tried to make it perfectly clear that the events of the day were not acceptable, and that the United States was not pleased with the aggressive behavior of Germany and Italy. In the letter, he said: "On a previous occasion I have addressed you on behalf of the settlement of political, economic, and social problems by peaceful methods and without resort to arms. But the tide of events seems to have reverted to the threat of arms . . . all the world, victor nations, vanquished nations, and neutral nations, will suffer."

Hitler did not answer this letter directly. Instead, he took up the subject in a speech that was broadcast across Germany. In reply to FDR's request that international problems be solved at the council table, Hitler declared that the greatest conference in the world, the League of Nations, was created "in accordance with the will of an American president." He then correctly noted that the first country not to join was the United States. Hitler explained that he was only following the United States' example when Germany dropped out of the League of Nations "after years of purposeless participation." In his speech, Hitler mocked Roosevelt, saying he, Hitler, had a much more difficult time with Germany than Roosevelt did with the United States.

"THE POINT IN HISTORY AT WHICH WE STAND IS FULL OF PROMISE AND DANGER. THE WORLD WILL EITHER MOVE FORWARD TOWARD UNITY AND WIDELY SHARED PROSPERITY—OR IT WILL MOVE APART."
—Franklin D. Roosevelt

"Mr. Roosevelt!" Hitler said, "I fully understand that the vastness of your nation and the immense wealth of your country allow you to feel responsible for the history of the whole world and for the history of all nations. I, sir, am placed in a much more modest and smaller sphere."

Despite the speech, Hitler was actually too busy planning his strategy to dominate all of Europe to listen to pleas for peace. Hitler's next goal was a conquest of Poland. Parts of Poland had once belonged to Germany during the period of the great Prussian Empire in the 19th century. Hitler, eager to have it back, would be happy to obtain the rest of Poland as an added prize. In order to accomplish this, Hitler got the Soviet Union (the large nation that broke up into many smaller countries, including Russia, during the early 1990s) to agree to a non-aggression pact in August 1939. That way, when the Germans attacked Poland, the Russians would do nothing to stop them.

1939 World's Fair

A pleasant diversion from all the conflict was the world's fair at Flushing Meadow Park in New York City. Groundbreaking was in June 1936, and the 1,200-acre fair opened in May 1939. President Roosevelt attended the opening day and was the first president to appear on television, a new invention that was featured at the fair. The centerpieces of the fair were the 700-foot-high tower called the Trylon and a 200-foot-diameter globe called the Perisphere.

One exhibit was put on in honor of the WPA to show what "The American Way" did for the country in putting three million people to work over the previous six years. There were models of bridges and buildings and other WPA achievements, as well as performances by actors and musicians, and demonstrations by other WPA-employed workers such as a weaver and a model maker.

Dozens of countries had exhibits at the fair. Conspicuously missing from the country exhibits was Germany, though Italy and Japan did have exhibits. FDR said about the world's fair that it would be "a memorable and historic fair, one that will profoundly influence our national life for many years to come" and that it was "an inspiring thing for nations and communities to have high objectives, to unite their energies in self-appraisal, and boldly plan for the future. The New York World's Fair is a challenge to all Americans who believe in the destiny of this nation."

The League of Nations had its own exhibit. The fair organizers knew that Americans were still wary of the League. According to the carefully worded "World's Fair Guide," the exhibit "makes no false claims, issues no propaganda or false pleadings."

Technology was a big theme at the fair. Companies such as Hoover (vacuum cleaners), Bakelite Corporation (plastics), Westinghouse (appliances), and Chrysler Motors (automobiles) exhibited their latest inventions and their visions for their future products.

A Royal Visit

The idea for a British royal visit to the United States was first born in 1937, at the suggestion of the American actor and Roosevelt family friend Douglas Fairbanks Jr. (he had played with FDR Jr. in New York's Central Park when they were kids). A strong believer in the importance of Anglo-American relations during the looming crisis, Fairbanks felt it was important for the two countries to maintain close ties. Through Fairbanks's efforts, the seeds for a royal visit were planted on both sides of the Atlantic Ocean. It was just a matter of when the visit could occur.

When FDR found out that Great Britain's King George VI and Queen Elizabeth were planning to visit Canada in 1939, he wrote a letter to the king asking him to consider stopping in the United States. He said, "I need not assure you that it would give my wife and me the greatest pleasure to see you, and, frankly, I think it would be an excellent thing for Anglo-American relations if you could come visit the United States." FDR sent the letter to Ambassador Kennedy in London and asked him to deliver it to the king. He also said he would be delighted if the king and queen brought their children, who could play with FDR's grandchildren.

King George wrote back that he would be delighted to visit, but as he did not want to stay out of England too long, the visit would have to be brief. He said the children (including the 13-year-old future queen, Elizabeth II) were too young to make the demanding trip. The plan was for the royals to arrive the first week of June. At first, FDR had in mind a relaxing few days at Hyde Park, but soon a busy schedule was planned for the royal couple. FDR got very involved in planning the details

of the royal visit. He wanted the American public to sympathize with Great Britain.

FDR's son James Roosevelt traveled to England in 1939 to visit with the royal family and firm up details about their visit to the United States. On June 7, 1939, the king and queen arrived at Niagara Falls (the border of New York State and Canada). They proceeded by

Douglas Fairbanks Jr. (right) in *The Corsican Brothers* (1941), the last film he made before going into the service.

Eleanor Roosevelt, King George VI, Sara Delano Roosevelt, Queen Elizabeth, and FDR, June 1939.

train for the approximately 12-hour trip to Washington, D.C. There, they were officially received by President Roosevelt and Mrs. Roosevelt, the vice president and his wife, and members of the cabinet.

The king and queen got to do some sightseeing in the nation's capital, and had several meals at the White House and the British Embassy. On June 9, they had lunch with the Roosevelts aboard a ship, and the king laid a wreath at George Washington's tomb at Mount Vernon, Virginia. That night, they left by train for New York, where they visited the world's fair. While in the city, the king and queen visited Columbia University, then headed by train north to Hyde Park.

They had dinner at Hyde Park with the Roosevelts that evening. FDR made a rousing toast to their majesties: "I am persuaded that the greatest single contribution our two countries have been enabled to make to civilization, and to the welfare of peoples throughout the world, is the example we have jointly set by our manner of conducting relations between our two nations."

While at Hyde Park, the king and the president swam at the pool, but disappointed photographers were asked not to take photographs of the leaders in their bathing suits.

On Sunday, June 11, a highly publicized picnic for the British monarchs was held. The menu included hot dogs, smoked turkey, Virginia ham, salad, cranberry sauce, and rolls, with strawberry shortcake for dessert. FDR's mother was not pleased that lowly hot dogs were on the menu, but the king and queen did not seem to mind.

The king later wrote of his conversations with FDR while in America: "I had two good conversations with the president, besides many opportunities of informal talks on current matters in the car driving with him. He

Memories of Eleanor Roosevelt

BY ROBERT MORGENTHAU,
Manhattan district attorney and son of FDR's treasury secretary, Henry Morgenthau Jr.

"Mrs. Roosevelt would cook. She used to like to have these cookouts at Val-Kill. And when the president came with the king [George VI] and queen [Elizabeth] of England [in June 1939], I was cooking the hot dogs.

Mrs. Roosevelt, of course, was really his [the president's] eyes and ears. She got out in the country and listened and reported back. She was a very important part of his administration. And my mother [Elinor Morgenthau] used to travel with her. Down in the coal mines of West Virginia and all over the country. My mother used to have to go to bed for a couple of days after she got back, because she wasn't as physically strong as Mrs. Roosevelt."

was very frank and friendly, and seemed genuinely glad that I had been able to pay him this visit."

The royal visit in 1939 set the stage for the closest relationship between the United States and Great Britain in over 150 years. Besides showing hospitality to the royal family, FDR soon became very friendly with Winston Churchill, who was the British prime minister during the war.

Hitler Invades Poland

Early on the morning of September 1, 1939, FDR was awakened by a phone call from his ambassador to France, William Bullitt. He turned on his light and listened. The news was grim—the German army had just invaded Poland. FDR made a few phone calls to some of his cabinet members. The news spread fast from one advisor to another. FDR, with his nerves of steel, got a couple more hours of sleep before another phone call aroused him. It was Bullitt again, reporting about his conversation with the French government. The French believed that they and England must assist Poland. FDR listened carefully, hung up, and went back to sleep briefly for a final time before taking a call from Ambassador Joseph Kennedy in London. A dejected Kennedy was calling to tell FDR about his conversation with the British prime minister. FDR had his breakfast and contemplated the newly complicated world situation.

The next days were very busy for FDR and his cabinet. FDR got opinions from his advisors about ways in which the United States could help England and France without actually going to war. Unlike Germany, England and France had not been arming themselves in preparation for war. Their military strengths were not up to par with that of Germany. FDR talked to his cabinet about how the war in Europe would affect America, and what could be done about it.

Meanwhile, Poland suffered. The poorly prepared country was no match for the firepower of the Germans. The Polish fought back as best they could, but it did not do much good. On the morning of September 3, FDR was again awakened by a phone call at four o'clock in the morning. It was Ambassador Kennedy calling to inform the president that Great Britain was about to declare war on Germany.

After the British and French declared war on Germany, President Roosevelt declared that the United States was remaining neutral. He was dismayed by the events in Poland, but he was not ready to bring the United States into the war. A national poll taken that month showed that 67 percent of Americans wanted the country to stay completely neutral, while only 2.5 percent wanted America to enter the war at that point.

On September 23, 1939, a conference began in Panama. FDR sent his undersecretary of state, Sumner Welles. The nations of North, Central, and South America got together and discussed how the war would affect the economy, stability, and security of the Americas. The countries agreed to cooperate and help each other.

Then, the Soviet Union attacked Finland in November 1939. The winter of 1939 was full of uncertainty for the people of the United States. In January 1940, FDR wrote a letter to Crown Prince Olav of Norway. He said: "I think every day of the very difficult situation in which the Scandinavian countries find themselves, especially since the brutal attack on Finland. The only ray of light is the magnificent defense that is being put up by Finland." He said he was sorry that the United States could not do more and that the isolationists would offer sympathy but little else.

FDR felt it was time for a last-ditch effort at establishing peace in Europe. He sent Sumner Welles to Europe in February 1940. Welles first went to Italy to meet with Mussolini. The Italian leader was presented with a letter from President Roosevelt. When Mussolini read it, he smiled. He told Welles that he had long wanted to meet with Roosevelt and hoped it would soon happen.

In early March 1940, Welles went to Germany to meet with Hitler. FDR had not written a letter to Hitler, nor did he have any particular agreement or truce for Welles to put on the table. FDR only wanted Welles to probe Hitler's mind and discover his intentions. The German leader told Welles that he only wanted to claim for Germany those parts of Europe that had a heavily German population. He said that he wanted nothing to do with Great Britain or any other non-German parts of Europe, so long as those countries would leave Germany alone. He felt war was being forced upon him.

Invasion of France

Unfortunately, Hitler's words were not to be trusted. As the spring flowers bloomed in 1940, Hitler's war machine went into action again. Thus ended what was known as the "phony war," the period of tense inactivity between fall 1939 and spring 1940. Denmark and Norway were invaded on April 9, and soon fell to the Germans. The same fate awaited Holland, Belgium, Luxembourg, and France in the nerve-wracking months of May and June. Though publicly FDR would not acknowledge that America would enter the war, in his heart, he knew the likelihood of America remaining neutral was growing slimmer. On May 16, FDR asked Congress for $1.1 billion to spend on defense, and just two weeks later he asked for another $1.2 billion.

As the Germans began to bomb Great Britain, millions of British people (many of them children) were evacuated to the countryside. Like Churchill, FDR greatly admired the resolve and bravery of the British people. This, no doubt, increased his desire to lend aid to the British. He also had a feeling that if the Germans defeated Britain, it would spell disaster.

In July 1940, after much of Western Europe had fallen to the Germans, FDR went back to Congress and asked for more money—another $4.8 billion for defense. Despite the United States' neutrality, FDR's philosophy was that "partial defense is inadequate defense. . . . We cannot defend ourselves a little here and a little there." This closely echoed his words during World War I. By this time, factories were busy producing tanks, ships, and planes by the thousands. Yet, in the summer of 1940, FDR still insisted that he would not send American men to take part in a European war. He was only trying to provide an adequate defense for his country against attack. The president's situation was tricky. It was hard to please the isolationists and the warmongers. Before war's end, FDR would be accused of both giving in to Hitler and leading America into war.

Meanwhile, the situation became still more complicated. In June 1940, the Soviet Union occupied Latvia and Estonia, and in September 1940, Italy invaded Egypt and the British sent troops to Africa in response. It was quickly becoming a worldwide war.

The presidential election of 1940 was approaching, and FDR had to decide what to do about it. Eight years had already gone by in a flash. No other president had ever served more than eight years in office. What was FDR to do?

When Friends Turn into Enemies

Not long after his second election in 1936, FDR had told an audience he would be happy to turn over the presidency to someone else in 1941. In fact, he had plans for his retirement in 1941, and dreamed of what he would do with his free time at Hyde Park. He had so many hobbies and such a great love for nature that he knew he would enjoy retirement immensely.

As the election of 1940 approached, however, FDR's view on the matter changed. He noted the critical nature of the crises facing the world. He would not push himself into the

By spring 1940, the German army had reached Holland.

nomination, but if he was called overwhelmingly, he would serve. Eleanor was against FDR running again, and so were some of his

Memories of Henry A. Wallace

BY JEAN WALLACE DOUGLAS,
daughter of Vice President (1941–1945),
Secretary of Agriculture (1933–1941), and Secretary
of Commerce (1945–1947) Henry A. Wallace

"Roosevelt recognized my father's true interest in agriculture and the land. [Wallace's] father was also secretary of agriculture. He was never a politician, whereas so many people are. We were not a political family. He was never good in politics at all. He would say things the way they were, and in politics you're not supposed to do that. My father was a man of very few words. [He was] extremely intelligent. So intelligent I never quite understood the things he knew and did. Very few politicians ever had any idea of what he was talking about. Roosevelt always called my father 'old man common sense.' I think my father was one of the most intelligent vice presidents we've ever had. It's because I think he always looked 20 years ahead of himself. I think it was very hard for people to understand my father for that reason.

He realized the importance of our agriculture to the country, and especially during the war years. Well, they couldn't understand what happens when you have overproduction . . . you could never be a politician and look too far ahead. The average American is very shortsighted, and they just want it immediately, and they never look very far ahead."

former confidants. FDR's close friend and advisor James Farley was shocked and angered by Roosevelt's decision not to rule out a record third term in office. Farley felt two terms was enough for any president. He had also been eyeing his own chances at a run for the nation's highest office. Even Roosevelt was not certain he wanted to run for a third term.

Farley was not the only former Roosevelt supporter who turned against his old friend. By this time, FDR and his own vice president, John Nance Garner, had grown apart. By the time the 1930s drew to a close, they barely spoke to each other. In fact, Garner was also interested in running for president in 1940.

Despite the challenges from his former friends, Roosevelt was the overwhelming favorite during the Democratic National Convention in the summer of 1940. On the first ballot, he got 946 votes, far more than needed for a two-thirds majority. Second place went to James Farley, with only 72 votes. Third place went to Vice President Garner with 61 votes. FDR was satisfied with the results. America wanted him back. Now it was just a question of who would be his vice presidential running mate. After a long struggle in the convention hall, the selection of longtime secretary of agriculture Henry A. Wallace was finally made. Roosevelt was pleased at the choice. Wallace was still one of his most trusted advisors.

FDR's acceptance speech that evening explained his position on a third term:

"Eight years in the Presidency, following a period of bleak depression, and covering one world crisis after another, would normally entitle any man to the relaxation that comes from honorable retirement. . . . Today all private plans, all private lives, have been in a sense repealed by an overriding public danger . . . my conscience will not let me turn my back upon a call to service.

The right to make that call rests with the people through the American method of a free election. Only the people themselves can draft a President."

In his own acceptance speech, vice-presidential nominee Wallace called the Republicans the party of appeasement toward Hitler. FDR himself did not really go on a campaign swing in 1940, since, as he put it, "any president with any normal sense would be compelled to be close to Washington in case of an emergency." His son FDR Jr. was actively involved in campaigning to young Democrats; he gave 300 speeches in support of FDR's bid for a third term.

Franklin Roosevelt's Republican opponent in 1940 was Wendell Willkie. FDR was somewhat hurt that some major newspapers came out in favor of Willkie in 1940. He felt that Willkie was a strong candidate. Willkie looked for angles to attack FDR. He tried various themes, including the lack of progress of the New Deal, and the controversy of an unprecedented third term in office. But Willkie seemed to make the biggest dent in FDR's lead in the polls when he accused Roosevelt of leading the country down the path to war. By 1940, there were millions of Americans who were against Roosevelt and his policies. In fact, most people either loved FDR or hated him. Few Americans had no opinion about their leader.

Though FDR did little campaigning at first, Willkie's accusations finally angered him, and he fought back as the election neared. He was not willing to sit back and let Willkie decide the tone of the election campaign.

As it turned out, with all the unrest in the world, the mtajority of Americans were simply not willing to take a chance on someone new. By a margin of 449 to 82 electoral votes, FDR was elected to a record third term in November 1940. Though the Election Day results were in his favor, it was not quite a landslide in the popular vote (27 million to 22 million). Shortly after the election, FDR wrote a letter to his speechwriter and friend Samuel Rosenman in which he said about the election, "In many ways it was a narrow escape—not for

Campaign buttons for and against FDR, 1940.

personalities but for ideals . . . I have learned a number of things which make me shudder—because there were altogether too many people in high places in the Republican campaign who thought in terms of appeasement of Hitler."

FDR decided to meet with Wendell Willkie for the sake of unity in the country, which FDR felt might be very important during the next four years. Surprisingly, upon talking with Willkie, FDR discovered that he liked and respected the man, and he even offered Willkie a position in his administration. Willkie eased off his isolationist views after the election. He respected Roosevelt, and served as a diplomat, visiting the Soviet Union and China on behalf of the U.S. government before his untimely death in October 1944.

⇒ Collect Roosevelt Stories

ANYONE YOU KNOW who was born before 1938 probably has some memory of FDR—hearing him on the radio, seeing him on a newsreel, or reading about him in the newspapers. As you will see from the recollections throughout this book, these memories can be interesting. Though you most likely won't find anyone who actually met FDR, you will find plenty of people who remember him distinctly.

YOU'LL NEED
★ Tape recorder
★ Computer or notebook and pen

Ask people who would be old enough to remember the FDR era if you can interview them briefly. What questions would you ask of someone who lived through FDR's presidency? You could ask them if they remember any of his fireside chats on the radio or remember his New Deal programs. Do they remember hearing his "day of infamy" speech and what they felt at the time? Do they remember hearing about his death? You might be surprised that some people think they have nothing to contribute, but if they were at least seven or eight years old when FDR died, they probably have some memory of him.

Using your tape recorder or notebook and pencil, record their memories. For each interview subject, write down their first name, year of birth, and where they lived at the time.

Format each memory on a separate sheet of paper and give each one a heading with a title. The title of the memory can be a quote from their story, or the topic they discuss. If you talk to enough people, you will have a nice scrapbook of firsthand memories of the Roosevelt era.

Neutral No More

The rapid deterioration of the world situation caused FDR to rethink his country's stingy policy on assisting other countries.

FDR had made a friend in Great Britain. The newly elected prime minister, Winston Churchill, was a man after FDR's heart. Like FDR, he had served in his country's navy. Churchill was a thinking man's politician—personable, strong, and determined. He and FDR exchanged letters and seemed to understand each other quite well. They addressed their letters to each other "Former Naval Person."

The United States had already sent Britain 100 outdated bombers, but of course that was just a drop in the bucket. In September 1940, FDR offered 50 old American destroyers in exchange for 99-year leases on some British-owned military bases in the Atlantic. FDR was excited about getting to operate bases in the Atlantic, and he told one opponent of the idea that he saw the deal as "the finest thing for the nation that has been done in your lifetime and mine." He added, "I am absolutely certain that this particular deal will not get us into war."

In December 1940, Churchill wrote to FDR to let him know that Britain would need a great many supplies to fight the war, and that they were coming to the end of their money.

In a passionate fireside chat in December 1940, known as the "arsenal of democracy" speech, FDR made a case to the American public for building America's own defenses. "We must have more ships, more guns, more planes—more of everything," he said.

"I want to make it clear that it is the purpose of the nation to build now with all possible speed every machine, every arsenal, every factory that we need to manufacture our defense material. . . . As planes and ships and guns and shells are produced, your government, with its defense experts, can then determine how best to use them to defend this hemisphere. The decision as to how much shall be sent abroad and how much shall remain at home must be made on the basis of our overall military necessities. We must be the great arsenal of democracy."

In his annual address to Congress on January 6, 1941, FDR spoke of an "unprecedented" moment in U.S. history. He truly felt that the security of the United States had never been as threatened as it was at that moment. The assault of the Germans "blotted out" democratic life in many countries. Though he acknowledged that industry and the military were working hard, he said he was not yet satisfied with the progress. In the most famous part of his speech, the president called out four essential freedoms that had to exist in the future:

"The first is freedom of speech and expression—everywhere in the world. The second is freedom of every person to worship God in his own way anywhere in the world. The third is freedom from want. . . . The fourth is freedom from fear. . . . The world order which we seek is the cooperation of free countries, working together in a friendly, civilized society."

Within the "four freedoms" speech was the seed of an idea that FDR would later develop further—into an organization called the United Nations. It was now inevitable that the United States would end its neutrality. The world was in peril. FDR knew the United States had to act soon.

To show he was committed to helping defeat the Nazis, FDR came up with the idea of allowing Britain to borrow what it needed in order to fight the Germans. The so-called Lend-Lease Bill was introduced to Congress in January 1941. Finally in March 1941, the Lend-Lease Bill was approved in the Senate by a margin of 60–31. In June 1941, Germany

invaded Russia, breaking the non-aggression pact the two countries had made.

By the summer of 1941, FDR decided that U.S. troops should occupy Iceland and Greenland in order to strengthen the United States' presence in the Atlantic. Slowly, the United States and England began to discuss a possible strategy for winning the war. Both Roosevelt and Churchill thought that naval and air power would win the war. Neither favored the idea of a land war on the European continent. Secretary of Commerce Harry Hopkins was sent to Moscow to meet with Joseph Stalin and get his impression of the German army's strength.

In August 1941, President Roosevelt met with Winston Churchill off the coast of Newfoundland, Canada. The two leaders agreed to an eight-point program, a joint declaration of their countries' beliefs called the Atlantic Charter. They stated that all nations should be allowed to have democracy. They agreed that neither the United States nor the United Kingdom sought any territory or other gain from the war. They also agreed to cooperate with each other and declared that all nations had to stop using force, so peace could exist again.

FDR's words became harsh. He was furious that Hitler was threatening American ships in the Atlantic. In October 1941, he said,

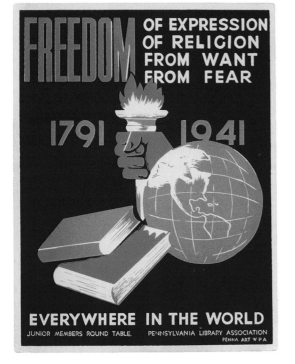

A poster celebrating FDR's "four freedoms."

⟹ Perform an Abbott and Costello–Style Routine

ABBOTT AND COSTELLO were the most popular comedians of the war years. Their quick banter was perfect for radio, the vaudeville stage, and the movies. In this activity, you'll perform the type of routine that Abbott and Costello and other fast-talking comedians might have performed during the early 1940s. Comedy is all about timing. Pacing the lines and making the audience anticipate the next line is what makes their routines work. Practice until you have the timing and tone right. Hint: The "Abbott" character's tone is exasperated, while "Costello"'s is naive.

YOU'LL NEED
★ The script below
★ Friend
★ An audience

C: I'm going to be president!

A: You can't become president just like that. You have to run.

C: Why do I have to run? Can't I walk?

A: No, run for office.

C: I have to run to the office?

A: You can walk while you run, or you can sit still. But you have to run.

C: I don't get it.

A: Look, if you want to be president, you have to have a platform.

C: Do I have to build it myself?

A: If you want to run, you need something to run on. That's why you have a platform.

C: How big is this platform going to be?

A: Stop talking nonsense.

C: Well, say I have the platform, what else do I need to be president?

A: Well, once you have a platform, you need a debate.

C: A what?

A: Debate, debate.

C: Da bait? What, am I going fishing? I might as well, while I'm standing on my platform.

A: Now, cut it out. If you want to be president, you'll need a running mate.

C: A running mate?

A: Yes, of course.

C: Why can't I run by myself?

A: You need a running mate in case something happens to you. You could drop dead.

C: I better not run very fast, it sounds dangerous.

A: Listen, if something happens while you're president, your mate will take over.

C: Leave my wife out of this.

A: Not that mate. Your running mate.

C: How many mates do I have?

A: You're being silly. If you want to be president, you'll have to campaign.

C: Campaign?

A: Of course.

C: How about let's save the campaign until after I win? I don't want to celebrate too early.

A: You're too dumb. Didn't you go to school, stupid?

C: Yeah, and I came out the same way.

"We will not let Hitler prescribe the waters of the world on which our ships may travel. The American flag is not going to be driven from the seas either by his submarines, his airplanes, or his threats."

Though the United States was officially neutral throughout most of 1941, men were enlisting in the armed forces by the thousands, and the country seemed poised for war. In fact, in November 1941, the government asked Universal Studios to put a rush on the release of a new Abbott and Costello comedy called *Keep 'Em Flying,* a film about what happens when the two screen clowns join the air corps. The pair had already made successful films about joining the army and the navy earlier in 1941. For the filming of *Keep 'Em Flying,* the army loaned out 175 war planes and the use of the Cal-Aero Academy in California. The government felt films like this had a positive impact on the recruitment effort and the spirit of the nation.

Pearl Harbor

Europe was not the only area of the world where major trouble was brewing. Since the 1930s, problems had been plaguing the Far East. It started in 1931, when Japanese troops had invaded a part of China called Manchuria. The Japanese kept pushing further into China and gaining control over more territory. In 1940, Japan agreed to an alliance with Germany and Italy. This did not bode well for Japan's relations with the United States. Though officially neutral, the United States was warning these other countries against aggression.

Though the United States tried diplomacy with Japan, it failed. On December 7, 1941, more than 350 Japanese planes launched a surprise attack on the U.S. naval base Pearl

FDR signs the declaration of war against Japan, December 1941.

Harbor on the island of Oahu, Hawaii. There were massive casualties; about 3,000 people lost their lives. Dozens of American ships were sunk, and many airplanes were destroyed on the runways where they sat.

The next day, President Roosevelt had no choice but to ask Congress to declare war on Japan. His speech to Congress on December 8, 1941, was destined to become famous once he uttered the words: "Yesterday, December 7, 1941, a date which will live in infamy. The United States of America was suddenly and deliberately attacked by naval and air forces of the Empire of Japan." The word *infamy* had not been his first choice, but it turned out to make a lasting impression on most Americans. A declaration of war against Germany and Italy soon followed. Suddenly, the United States found itself an ally of Stalin, the fearsome leader of the Soviet Union. FDR was not thrilled to be dealing with the Soviets, but now any enemy of Germany was a friend of the United States.

Italy, Germany, and Japan joined together to form the Axis powers. They were pitted against the Allies—consisting mainly of the United States, the Soviet Union, and England, but aided by a supporting cast of many other countries, including the "underground" French resistance, who were trying to fight the Germans from occupied France.

Remembering Pearl Harbor

BY PETER PROMMERSBERGER,
son of German immigrants

"My earliest memory of the time of World War II came on a Sunday afternoon in early December. My father and I were in the basement setting up a model train table in anticipation of Christmas. The announcement came over the radio about the attack on Pearl Harbor. From the shocked reaction of my parents, I knew that there would be a change in what was a nice, peaceful life.

Everyone waited for the U.S. reaction. Shortly after came the now famous 'day of infamy' speech by FDR. Since I had grandparents and extended family in Germany, worry and fear became a constant in our lives."

Memories of FDR

BY THEODORE KHEEL,
executive director of the National War Labor Board, 1944–1945

"I was in awe of Roosevelt. The respect he had in the country was tremendous. The atmosphere of the public feeling about the war against Adolf Hitler was much different than it is about the war now [in Iraq]. There was virtually nobody who was not in favor of the war. People would join the army, navy or marines voluntarily. The extent to which people wanted to go to war to save the world from the Nazis was so different. I remember very well the spirit of America."

Memories of FDR

BY MATTHYS LEVY,
immigrated to the United States as a child

"When I arrived as a ten-year-old in the United States in 1939, FDR was president and remained so during the war years until his untimely death in 1945. He was the image of the presidency, and I remember clearly thinking that he had always been the president and that no one else could possibly replace him. Curiously, I have no image of him as suffering from a physical problem but saw him as a vigorous older person with a strong and distinctive voice. The voice was one of his most unique characteristics, clear, well modulated, and easily understandable. Since I learned English during this period, his manner of speaking was the one I wanted to imitate, rather than the coarser-sounding street voices I heard in my New York neighborhood. I looked forward to hearing him as he delivered his weekly fireside chats.

As a leader, he seemed to me to be unbeatable. When I heard him deliver his speech to the Congress on December 8, 1941, the words and expressions seemed Shakespeare-like, and the call to arms made me feel, oh, how I wished I were old enough to join the fight! It is difficult, having lived through the subsequent wars, with their questionable causes, to remember how there was no question at the start of the great war that one should be joined to the conflict. The enemy was clearly evil and our cause, clearly good. No war since then has had the same inevitable clarity. To a great extent, it was the communications from Roosevelt that provided the vision and the clarity of purpose. As I remember them, FDR's detractors seemed mean and narrow-minded and clearly lacked the patrician bearing that made FDR so powerful a leader."

Franklin D. Roosevelt now joined Abraham Lincoln and Woodrow Wilson as a wartime president. Before long, the government implemented the draft. Men had to register with their local draft board and were selected at random for military service. Millions of men were drafted into the army, navy, and marines.

Sara Roosevelt Dies

A president is not alone very often. This is even truer for a wartime president. There is almost always someone close at hand, whether it is an advisor or a security agent. Still, that does not mean a president cannot feel lonely and isolated. By the early 1940s, FDR was feeling lonelier than he had in his life.

His mother, Sara, had been the one person he could count on for emotional support through his entire life. FDR adored and respected her. The American public loved Sara Delano Roosevelt too. She was in the public eye more than any other presidential mother in history, making appearances at events and praising her son in the press.

By the end of 1940, she was 86 years old, and her health was failing. She hung on for much of 1941, but on September 7, 1941, Sara Delano Roosevelt died in Hyde Park, in the same room where she had given birth to her only child. FDR was there to say good-bye. He was deeply saddened by her death and wore a black armband in mourning for her for several months. A few weeks later, Eleanor's brother Hall Roosevelt died. Also in 1941, FDR's long-time secretary and friend Missy LeHand had a severe stroke and could not work for him anymore.

Eleanor was supportive during FDR's time of mourning for his mother, but she was simply not around very much during the war years. When she was not traveling around the country visiting military hospitals, she was making trips overseas. She enjoyed traveling and felt it was helpful to the morale of the soldiers. In 1942, she visited the royal family in England. In August 1943, Eleanor traveled to the southwest Pacific, on a trip that spanned 23,000 miles and took her to New Zealand, Australia, and Guadalcanal. Then, in 1944, she went on a trip to visit American soldiers on duty in various places south of the United States. On that journey she stopped in Puerto Rico, Antigua, Trinidad, Recife, Panama, Guatemala, Jamaica, and Cuba.

Winning the Home Front War

Just as important as winning the war on the battlefield was winning the war on the home front. Thousands and then millions of Ameri-

Eleanor Roosevelt during a trip to Central and South America, 1944.

cans left their homes (some voluntarily and some through the draft) to help the war effort. Automobile factories shut down their car-making operations and switched to making jeeps, tanks, and munitions. Women took over factory positions that were vital to the war effort when millions of American men left their jobs to fight the war. FDR excelled as a leader on the home front. His optimism was a beacon of hope for all Americans.

Everyday items that Americans had enjoyed before the war were now scarce. Rubber, metal, and gasoline were in high demand for tanks, battleships, and bombers but low supply for the American public.

> **"THE ONLY LIMIT TO OUR REALIZATION OF TOMORROW WILL BE OUR DOUBTS OF TODAY."**
>
> —Franklin D. Roosevelt

Millions of parents, sisters, brothers, and wives across the country worried about the men who were fighting a war thousands of miles away. In 1942, the FDR administration introduced a free and efficient way to get letters back and forth between soldiers and their families and friends. Once a letter to or from a soldier was written, it was microfilmed. Two thousand pounds of so-called v-mail letters could fit on 25 pounds of microfilm, saving precious cargo space.

FDR's main job on the home front was to keep the morale high and calm the public's fears. In reality, he had already been doing that for years, with his New Deal programs and his fireside chats and other speeches. The New Deal had put people to work and helped them feel useful and thankful toward their government. Americans took this spirit of renewal to the war. It helped that the majority of Americans already trusted and believed FDR completely, based on his first eight years in office.

In a fireside chat given on February 23, 1942, Roosevelt told the American people what he expected from them during the war:

"Here are three high purposes for every American:

1. We shall not stop work for a single day. If any dispute arises we shall keep on working while the dispute is solved by mediation, or conciliation or arbitration—until the war is won. 2. We shall not demand special gains or special privileges or special advantages for any one group or occupation. 3. We shall give up conveniences and modify the routine of our lives if our country asks us to do so. We will do it cheerfully, remembering that the common enemy seeks to destroy every home and every freedom in every part of our land."

In April 1942, FDR submitted to Congress a seven-point program created to help keep costs down and help America win the war. As FDR said in his fireside chat of April 28:

"First. We must, through heavier taxes, keep personal and corporate profits at a low reasonable rate. Second. We must fix ceilings on prices and rents. Third. We must stabilize wages. Fourth. We must stabilize farm prices. Fifth. We must put more billions into War Bonds. Sixth. We must ration all essential commodities, which are scarce. Seventh. We must discourage installment buying, and encourage paying off debts and mortgages."

Even more difficult than making Americans feel good, FDR had to make the wartime government function properly. In 1942, the

Roosevelt administration put rationing into effect. Each American family was limited to a certain amount of meat, sugar, butter, and other scarce items per month. They had to trade in their ration tokens before being allowed to buy these items. With scarcity, there was the potential for outrageous prices, so FDR created the Office of Price Administration (OPA) to protect the consumer by creating price ceilings on certain items.

In May 1943, FDR reported that "So far, we have not been able to keep the prices of some necessities as low as we should have liked to keep them. . . . Wherever we find that prices of essentials have risen too high, they will be brought down. Wherever we find that price ceilings are being violated, the violators will be punished."

During wartime, it was also very important to keep the workforce operating smoothly. Labor disputes or strikes could be costly. FDR created the National War Labor Board to regulate wages and mediate disputes. The staff of the board consisted of skilled negotiators and lawyers. The War Labor Board was very successful in reducing the number of hours lost to strikes; if they happened at all they tended to be very brief. Congress even gave the president the authority to take over a plant or factory if a strike did not end. FDR had an enemy in labor leader John L. Lewis.

⇒ Ration a Meal

RATIONING OF MEAT, butter, sugar, and canned fruits and vegetables meant that Americans had to be creative in their cooking. Not only were families limited in the amounts of rationed goods they could buy every month, stores were often short of these rationed items. In this activity, you'll make a delicious dinner that is low on meat, butter, and sugar.

Adult supervision required

Modest Meatloaf
YOU'LL NEED
- ★ Oven
- ★ Large mixing bowl
- ★ ½ pound ground beef
- ★ 2 cups cubed bread
- ★ 1 cup seasoned bread crumbs or crushed, seasoned croutons
- ★ 1 teaspoon dried parsley
- ★ Pinch of salt
- ★ Pinch pepper
- ★ 1 egg, beaten
- ★ ¼ cup whole milk
- ★ ¼ cup ketchup
- ★ Metal or glass loaf pan or baking dish
- ★ Oven mitts

Preheat oven to 350 degrees. Mix all ingredients together in the large bowl. Spoon the mixture into the loaf pan or baking dish and shape into a loaf. Make sure there is some room around the meatloaf for the juices to accumulate. Cover with aluminum foil. Using oven mitts, place the pan in the middle of the oven and cook for 45 minutes. Remove the foil and continue cooking for 15 minutes. Test for doneness by poking a fork into the middle of the meatloaf. If the juices run clear, not pink, it is ready. Remove the pan from the oven and let the meatloaf sit for a few minutes before you eat it.

Poached Pears with Honey
YOU'LL NEED
- ★ 3 whole pears, peeled and quartered
- ★ Pot of water
- ★ Large serving bowl
- ★ ¼ cup honey
- ★ 1 tablespoon cinnamon

Cook the pears in a small pot of boiling water until they are tender. Carefully drain the water and allow the pears to cool for 10 minutes. Drizzle honey over the pears and stir gently. Let pears sit for 10 minutes, then place them into the serving bowl and sprinkle with cinnamon.

In one of his fireside chats, FDR explained to Americans what needed to be done to create an efficient labor force. He said,

"[W]e shall be compelled to stop workers from moving from one war job to another as a matter of personal preference; to stop employers from stealing labor from each other; to use older men, and handicapped people, and more women, and even grown boys and girls, wherever possible and reasonable. . . . The school authorities in all the states should work out plans to enable our high school students to take some time from their school year, (and) to use their summer vacations, to help farmers raise and harvest their crops, or to work somewhere in the war industries. . . . People should do their work as near their homes as possible. We cannot afford to transport a single worker into an area where there is already a worker available to do the job.

In some communities, employers dislike to employ women. In others they are reluctant to hire Negroes. In still others, older men are not wanted. We can no longer afford to indulge such prejudices or practices."

The American public was encouraged to buy war bonds, which were basically loans to the government, to be paid back later with interest. Because so much money was needed so quickly to fund the war, defense bonds were the best way to raise the money. One easy way to buy bonds was to purchase 10-cent defense stamps to fill a defense stamp booklet. Once 187 stamps were in the book, it could be exchanged at a post office (with an extra

A defense savings bond stamp booklet.

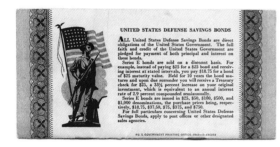

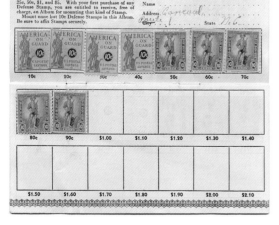

Saving for Bonds

During World War II, Americans bought war bonds, which helped the government pay for tanks, planes, and ammunition. A $20 war bond was worth a lot in the 1940s, when an average family earned $2,500 per year. During the war, $3.50 would buy a round of ammunition for an anti-tank gun, $2.50 would buy enough fuel to run a navy destroyer five miles, and $2 would buy 48 yards of barbed wire, or a blanket for a soldier.

nickel thrown in to make it worth $18.75) for a savings bond that would be worth $25 in 10 years. Entertainers traveled the country, making appearances to encourage Americans to buy bonds. FDR pushed the bonds in his fireside chats. These bond drives were very successful, and ultimately helped America win the war. By 1944, 81 million Americans had bought more than 600 million bonds.

The production of cars was suspended in 1942. The only active automobile makers during the war were Willys and American Bantam, who made the versatile army vehicle known as the Jeep. Many other automobile manufacturers quickly switched to defense production, building engines for millions of war-related vehicles, including tanks and airplanes. General Motors alone produced more than $12 billion of defense items for the Allies.

Americans seeking to purchase automobiles during the war had to be content with used models. Rubber shortages and gasoline rationing discouraged extensive driving or long trips. As FDR had said, sacrifices would be necessary to win the war.

Seemingly minor decisions by FDR during the war made a big difference to the American spirit. In January 1942, FDR wrote the "green light" letter to baseball commissioner Judge Kenesaw Landis. In the letter, he explained

⇒ Design a War Bond Poster

GOVERNMENT BONDS ARE simply loans from everyday citizens to the government that are paid back with interest years later. During war years, bonds are critical in helping the government pay for feeding, clothing, and arming the military. To promote bond sales during World Wars I and II, colorful posters were designed to appeal to the public's sense of patriotism. In this activity, you will design a war bond poster.

YOU'LL NEED
★ Poster board, 20 × 30 inches (or similar size)
★ Pencil
★ Ruler
★ Poster paints (a variety of colors)
★ Paint brushes (a variety of sizes)

Common images on war bond posters included eagles, Uncle Sam, soldiers, flags, fighter planes, tanks. Besides artwork, the posters also contained short tag lines, for example "Bonds Build Ships" (picture of ship) or "So We'll Meet Again, Buy More War Bonds" (picture of sailor waving) or "Keep Us Flying" (shows pilot in plane). Use a pencil to outline your ideas on the poster, and then paint a section at a time, allowing the top to dry, for example, before painting the middle. Remember to think big; make images that can be seen from a distance.

This savings bond poster was designed as part of a contest sponsored by the government in the 1930s.

that he thought the sport of professional base-ball should continue during the war. He said,

The National War Labor Board

BY THEODORE W. KHEEL,
executive director of the National War Labor Board, 1944–1945

"*I* was on the National Labor Relations Board as an attorney [1937], a job I was very pleased to get. Then, when the war broke out, Roosevelt first created the National Defense Labor Board to deal with disputes that would interfere with our effort to help the Allies. Shortly after Pearl Harbor, Congress passed legislation to allow the president to regulate prices and wages. By executive order, the president created the National War Labor Board (NWLB). It was charged with preventing strikes that interfered with the war effort and stabilizing wages because of the shortage of manpower and womanpower. I applied and became an attorney with the NWLB. There was such great pressure on what we were doing. The army would be in touch with us and say there's a strike at such and such factory, they're making armaments we need. Toward the end of its life [1944], I became executive director [of the NWLB], which was a presidential appointment. The president did become involved in a number of our disputes; one was with the department store Montgomery Ward. As a result of the decision we made, Montgomery Ward would not comply, and the president took control of the company. Sewell L. Avery [the head of Montgomery Ward] had to be carried out of the building. It was all over the front pages of the newspapers."

"I honestly feel that it would be best for the country to keep baseball going. There will be fewer people unemployed and everybody will work longer hours and harder than ever before. And that means that they ought to have a chance for recreation and for taking their minds off their work even more than before."

Though most teams were decimated by their best players going off to fight the war, the teams carried on as best they could. As Roosevelt noted, "Even if the actual quality to the teams is lowered by the greater use of older players, this will not dampen the popularity of the sport." One wartime team even had a one-armed pitcher. Also popular during the war years was a recently formed women's professional baseball league.

By 1940, American factories were buzzing with activity. Those men who were not on the battlefield were practically assured of jobs. Not only that, women were being employed in record numbers as well, doing jobs that were traditionally held by men such as working with heavy equipment and machinery. This was especially true in places such as Richmond, Virginia, where ships were being built and extra labor was needed.

As hundreds of thousands of tanks, planes, jeeps, and ships of all kinds were being built, the Depression disappeared. The war effort had shocked the economy back to life. Some critics of FDR have said that it is only because of the war that the Depression ended at all. However, it is not conceivable that the United States of 1933 would have been able to wage a winning war as did the United States of 1941. The country was already on its way to recovery by the time war broke out.

This famous poster came to represent Rosie the Riveter, a symbol of all the American women who entered the workforce during World War II.

Memories of FDR

BY SCHUYLER CHAPIN,
nephew of Francis Biddle (attorney general 1941–1945)

"When my uncle Francis Biddle was being sworn in as attorney general [in 1941], I was invited to the White House for the formal ceremony of his taking office. As I recall, we were in the president's study . . . It happened that Franklin Roosevelt knew my father (who had died about six months before) quite well. They went to the same college [Harvard]. They were in the Fly Club.

After Francis had been appointed officially, my Aunt Katherine motioned me to come over to Franklin's desk, which I did. We had a minute or two [long] conversation. I knew that my father was very fond of FDR, and FDR was very nice to me about my father. He made sympathetic comments about my father.

The most unforgettable thing was the size of the man from the waist up. When we shook hands, my hand was just swallowed up by his. He swung his wheelchair around from the desk to look me square in the eye. And then of course, when he wheeled around, you had these skinny legs, and shoes that had never been used. His legs were like two sticks. There was a little breeze in the White House, and you could see the wind flapping his pant legs. I tried to keep the look of surprise off my face. I don't know whether I succeeded or not. And of course his upper body was quite strong because he had specialized in trying to put himself in as good shape as possible. When we shook hands, I noticed his signet ring on his left hand, but it looked enormous, and I thought to myself, if that was on my hand, it would fall off. What struck me was the physical size of the man, at least from the waist up."

FDR at an army base in Washington, 1942.

6 FINAL VICTORIES

*F*DR's final years were consumed by World War II. It was an extremely complicated and costly war, fought on three continents. But Franklin Roosevelt had the tools he needed to be an effective wartime leader. He had been a key part of the navy department during World War I. He knew a great deal about mobilization, about naval warfare, and about supplies and weapons. Most important, FDR was a big-picture leader. He was able to digest what was happening around the country and around the world, and somehow coordinate everything. But in the end, it all took a terrible toll on him.

Progress in the War

After a pivotal Russian victory against the advancing Germans at Stalingrad in January 1942, FDR and other Allied leaders became more optimistic about their chances of a victory. With the Russians now on the offensive pushing the Germans back from the east, they felt sure that an attack from the west would apply pressure on the Germans.

In October 1942, FDR wrote a letter to King George VI of England in which he said the Allies were doing very well, and even though he did not expect victory in 1943, he felt the Axis had passed its peak and was in decline.

In January 1943, FDR and Churchill met at the Casablanca Conference in Morocco, Africa, to discuss the Allies' goals for 1943. Africa had been the first place American soldiers had made progress against the Germans. Among the things FDR and Churchill agreed upon at Casablanca was that nothing less than an unconditional surrender would be accepted from Germany and Japan. That meant there would be no negotiations or promises once Germany and Japan lost the war.

While at Casablanca, FDR met with General Dwight D. Eisenhower and discussed the good progress of the African campaign. FDR agreed that an invasion of Italy from the south (the island of Sicily) would have to come first in the spring and summer of 1943, before a more massive invasion of mainland Europe from across the English Channel.

During this time, Franklin Roosevelt began to plan for the peace that would follow the war. He knew from his experience in World War I that planning the peace needed as much attention as winning the war. In February 1943, the president said, referring to France,

Two snapshots of FDR taken by a soldier during the war.

"It is one of our war aims, as expressed in the Atlantic Charter, that the conquered populations of today be again the masters of their destiny. There must be no doubt anywhere that it is the unalterable purpose of the United Nations [the countries united against Germany and Japan] **to restore to the conquered peoples their sacred rights."**

Though it sounded simple, this statement meant a commitment of manpower and major involvement in postwar Europe.

By mid-1943, progress was being made in Italy. When General Eisenhower announced in September 1943 that Italy had surrendered, President Roosevelt warned people not to "settle back in your rocking chairs." He said, "The time for celebration is not yet. And I have a suspicion that when this war does end, we shall not be in a very celebrating mood."

In November 1943, FDR flew to Cairo, Egypt, to meet with Churchill and Chiang Kai-shek (the Chinese leader). Immediately after, he also met with Churchill and the Soviet Union leader Joseph Stalin in Tehran, Iran. The three leaders said, "The common understanding which we have here reached guarantees that victory will be ours." Then it was back to Cairo for FDR and Churchill for another conference, this time with the president of Turkey.

⇒ Make an Unbreakable, Double-Encoded Message

DURING WORLD WAR II, the Germans invented a unique code machine called "Enigma." The beauty of codes produced by this machine was that they were so sophisticated, they were nearly impossible to crack. Only the sender and receiver could calibrate their enigma machines to the same code frequency. FDR knew the importance of codes, and the United States had scientists working on them. In this activity you will make a sophisticated, double-secret code that nobody without the key can crack!

YOU'LL NEED
★ 2 kids
★ 104 index cards (52 for you and 52 for your friend)
★ Magic marker
★ Paper

First, in the center of each of 26 of your 52 index cards write a letter of the alphabet, starting with A. Next, at the top left of the Z card, write the number 1. On the top left of the A card write the number 2, at the top of the B card write the number 3, and keep numbering sequentially through the alphabet until you get to Y, which should be numbered 26 at the top left. This deck will be called the letter deck.

Have a friend do exactly the same thing with 26 of his cards. Now, in the center of each of your remaining 26 cards, write numbers, from 1 to 26. At the top left of the 26 card, write the letter A, and on the top left of the 1 card, write B. Continue until you get to the 25 card, and write the letter Z in the upper left corner. This will be called the number deck.

Have your friend do the same with the remaining 26 of his cards. Both of you should keep the number and letter decks separate.

Your friend should now go into another room with his two decks. Shuffle and mix each of your decks thoroughly. Deal out all your shuffled number deck cards. Next deal all your letter deck cards, each one above a number deck card. Keep dealing so you have 26 sets of letter and number cards laid out in front of you.

Translate the following message into code by finding each letter of the message among the letter cards laid out in front. Substitute the corresponding number on the number card you have dealt next to that letter card. Use a slash between each number. The message is: "This code cannot be cracked."

Now you need to give your friend the message, and a key with which to decipher the

code. The beauty of this code is that you have generated a random key by shuffling the decks. Your friend, who has the same decks, needs to duplicate the pattern you have made in order to read the message. This is where you use the little numbers and letters in the upper left corner of the index cards. These are the key to telling your friend how to organize his decks and decipher your message, without giving away the actual key itself in the process. Only the person who has the other deck will understand!

On a piece of paper, write the encoded message, followed by the key code. Write the pairs of small numbers and letters in the upper left corners of the 26 pairs. For example: 23/B 19/D 4/Z, etc. Your friend will then arrange his cards to match yours, and will be able to decode the message.

Anyone who intercepts the message will not be able to break the code!

> "WHEN YOU GET TO THE END OF YOUR ROPE, TIE A KNOT AND HANG ON."
>
> —Franklin D. Roosevelt

American troops wade ashore on D-Day, June 6, 1944

On June 5, 1944, FDR addressed the country with good news: "Yesterday, on June fourth, 1944, Rome fell to American and Allied troops. The first of the Axis capitals is now in our hands. One up and two to go!" To FDR, it was more than just a military victory. It was nothing less than the rescue of an ancient and historic center of culture from the grip of fascism. As FDR had written in a letter given to the American troops in Europe: "Never were the enemies of freedom more tyrannical, more arrogant, more brutal."

The good news kept coming. On the morning of June 6, 1944 (known as D-day), thousands of Allied troops had made a successful landing on the beaches of Normandy, France. The Germans were soon overpowered as wave after wave of Allied soldiers came ashore. Before long, the Nazis were on the retreat west through France. The Allies liberated Paris on August 24, 1944.

On the Eastern front, the Russian army was pushing through Poland and toward Germany. By the fall of 1944, it seemed inevitable to FDR that the European war would be won by the Allies. On September 5, American troops finally reached Germany. He knew that it was only a matter of time before the Allies and the Russians closed the vise on Germany.

As the fateful year of 1945 began, it was clear that there were still challenges ahead for the Allies. The war in Europe was nearing an end, but the outcome of the war in the Pacific was not as certain. Though General Douglas MacArthur had great success taking the Philippines from the Japanese in late 1944 and early 1945, there were other challenges. Major battles were still being fought. American forces were island hopping, trying to gain ground against the Japanese. The names of tiny, rocky, obscure Pacific islands were suddenly on the lips of people across America.

Host a Swing Dance Party

BIG BANDS AND swing music were popular throughout the war years and played a crucial role in keeping up morale both on the home front and with the troops. Swing music featured up-tempo melodies spiced with lots of clarinet and blazing drums. The beat was fun, and dances could be acrobatic as men swung their partners over their heads, across their backs, and under their legs. Many musicians traveled abroad to entertain the troops: The Andrews Sisters, Count Basie's Orchestra, Ella Fitzgerald, and Benny Goodman, to name a few. They often traveled with movie stars and comedians to put on shows for the soldiers. In this activity, you'll host a swing dance party.

YOU'LL NEED
★ A 45rpm record to trace
★ Sheets of black construction paper (one sheet per invite)
★ Pencil
★ Scissors
★ Coffee mug
★ Sheets of white paper (one sheet per invite)
★ All-purpose glue
★ Black thin-point marker
★ Record, CD, or tape player

★ Swing record albums, CDs, or tapes (see below for suggestions)
★ Paper plates, cups, and napkins
★ Fruit punch or other beverage
★ Snacks of your choice

Suggestions for music:
Artie Shaw "Begin the Beguine"
Glenn Miller "String of Pearls"
Jimmy Dorsey "Contrasts"
Andrews Sisters "Boogie Woogie Bugle Boy of Company B"
Duke Ellington "Take the A Train"
Stray Cats (modern-era swing) "Stray Cat Strut"

Create invitations by using a 45rpm record to trace a circle on each piece of black paper. Trace the center hole as well. Cut out the record-shaped invitations. Next, trace around the rim of a coffee mug on the white paper—one circle per invite—and then apply and trace the 45's center hole to the middle of each white circle. Cut these white circles out, also cutting the center holes out. These are your "record labels." Glue a label to the center of each black invitation record. Use the thin black markers to write "You're invited to a Swing Dance Party," along with the place and time of the party, on each label. You can host the party at your house or perhaps in the school gym, if that is possible.

Next, gather your big band and swing music. Ask your parents for help. You will want at least four different albums' worth of music.

The day of the party, prepare the drinks and snacks. You can be the DJ, or you can assign a friend or parent to do the honors. The DJ will listen to the music ahead of time and decide what songs to play and in what order.

When the party gets going, teach your guests the basic swing step. Here is one variation: A boy and a girl face each other and hold hands. The boy takes a slow step to his left while the girl takes a slow step to her right. Then the boy takes a slow step to his right and the girl a slow step to her left. Then the boy releases the girl's right hand from his left and takes a quick step back with his left foot, while the girl steps back with her right foot. They then rejoin hands and step back to their original starting position. This basic step can be embellished with a twirl or two and other improvisations. The best way to learn to dance to swing music is to let the music guide you. Follow the beat and the accents. You'll soon find yourself whirling across the dance floor.

General Eisenhower confers with troops in France, June 1944.

On the rocky island of Iwo Jima, the Americans defeated the Japanese in a fierce battle in February 1945. It did not look as though Japan would surrender anytime soon. Military strategists were talking about their options. FDR had earlier promised that "There are many roads that lead to Tokyo. We shall neglect none of them."

Meanwhile, in New Mexico, physicist Robert Oppenheimer and a team of American scientists were working on developing the atomic bomb for the United States to keep up with what Germany was thought to be secretly developing.

Memories of FDR

BY JOHN S. D. EISENHOWER,
son of General Dwight D. Eisenhower

"*F*ranklin D. Roosevelt was a nearly ideal war leader. His relations with his generals and admirals were very correct. They respected each other and avoided interfering in each other's business. It was Roosevelt's ability to inspire the people, the civilians, that was his greatest achievement. War is very hard on families—separation at best, serious wounding or death at worst. Yet Roosevelt's mixture of solemn dedication and utter optimism that we would win, his unfailing cheerfulness, kept the war popular even in the darkest of times."

Toward a United Nations

As early as 1943, FDR began to look ahead at postwar Europe with British leaders and with members of his own cabinet. FDR also thought about how Russia, Poland, Finland, Serbia, Austria, Hungary, and Germany should be handled at the end of the war. How would the nations of the world exist together after such a terrible war?

FDR began to speak of the Allies as a group of "united nations." He felt strongly that this group of nations should remain allied after the war. FDR also strongly believed that a European-only group after the war would not be enough. A worldwide body had to be formed.

The Allies of 1918 had not posed a united front after that war. Franklin could not help but think that if the United States had joined the League of Nations, it would have been more powerful, and possibly helped prevent another world war. This time American isolation would not be an option. FDR realized the world situation would be very complex. A defeated Germany and a surging Soviet Union would cause disarray in Europe. A powerful body of united nations had to emerge from the war.

At the Tehran Conference in 1943, Roosevelt, Stalin, and Churchill issued a declaration that talked about the future. The "big three" said:

"We shall seek the cooperation and active participation of all nations, large and small, whose peoples in heart and mind are dedicated, as are our own peoples, to the elimination of tyranny and slavery, oppression and intolerance. We will welcome them, as they may choose to come, into a world family of Democratic Nations."

In October 1944, FDR gave an important foreign policy speech in New York. He explained to his audience that the power the United States gained during the war brought with it the responsibility and opportunity "for leadership in the community of nations." In this speech he also gave his vision for how what he now called the Council of the United Nations would operate:

"The Council of the United Nations must have the power to act quickly and decisively to keep the peace by force, if necessary. A policeman would not be a very effective policeman if, when he saw a felon break into a house, he had to go to the Town Hall and call a town meeting to issue a warrant before the felon could be arrested. . . . The people of the Nation want their Government to act, and not merely to talk, whenever and wherever there is a threat to world peace."

Even after the election, FDR kept pushing this theme. In his inaugural speech in January 1945, he said, "We have learned to become citizens of the world, members of the human community."

In March 1945, FDR made a speech where he alluded to the mistake the United States made by not joining the League of Nations. He also tried to explain that the United Nations had to be a work in progress. He said:

"For the second time in the lives of most of us, this generation is face to face with the objective of preventing wars. To meet that objective, the nations of the world will either have a plan or they will not. The groundwork of a plan has now been furnished, and has been submitted to humanity for discussion and decision. No plan is perfect."

A conference was to be held in San Francisco at the end of April to lay the groundwork for organizing the United Nations. Though he would not live to see the United Nations, FDR had not only helped lay the foundation for it, he had made it clear the United States had to be a major part of the organization. With the United Nations becoming a reality, FDR had finally completed Woodrow Wilson's dream, the same dream FDR had campaigned for in 1920.

The Roosevelts Serve Their Country

FDR was proud that all four of his sons served their country during the war. Franklin D. Roosevelt Jr. joined the Naval Reserve in 1940 and was called for active duty in March 1941. He was an ensign in the navy and served in Europe, the Pacific, and North Africa. At one point he served as the chief officer of a destroyer that was bombed in Sicily, Italy. He received a Silver Star for bravery for trying to rescue one of his injured shipmates.

Elliott Roosevelt was an air force pilot who eventually became a brigadier general, in charge of more than 250 planes in the war in Africa, a fact that FDR was very proud of. John Roosevelt was a lieutenant commander in the navy, serving on an aircraft carrier.

James Roosevelt became a captain in the marine corps reserve starting in September 1939, and went on active duty in November 1940. He served in the Solomon and Gilbert Islands, and also took part in a raid on Makin Island in the Pacific Ocean. He received the Navy Cross and a Silver Star. In April 1942, FDR sent James around the world on a diplomatic mission. He visited the Philippines, China, Egypt, and Crete.

FDR did not see much of his sons during the war. He did get to see Elliott and FDR Jr., who had been granted special leave for that purpose, at the conference at Casablanca in 1943. Of all his children, FDR saw his daughter, Anna, most often during the war years. He also spent time with his grandchildren, especially at the holidays. By January 1945, FDR had 13 grandchildren ranging in age from toddler to 18. Anna Roosevelt Boettiger spent a lot of time living at the White House during 1944–1945 while her children Curtis and Eleanor were away at boarding school, and her

Memories of Franklin and Eleanor Roosevelt

BY ADELAIDE DOUGLAS KEY,
granddaughter of Josephus Daniels

"I played charades with Franklin and Eleanor Roosevelt. I was probably seven or eight years old. Their grandchildren were visiting and so we were invited over to the White House for dinner and to play with the grandchildren. Before dinner we played charades, and then after dinner Roosevelt and my father went off and did what they do. We continued to play after dinner. I got the spanking of my life because we were playing hide-and-seek. I was hiding behind these great big Chinese urns that were very valuable. I thought Franklin and Eleanor were wonderful. He had a wonderful, wonderful laugh, when he'd throw his head back and laugh."

husband John Boettiger was serving in the army. Anna served as White House hostess when her mother was traveling, and also offered advice and support to FDR.

Anna was no stranger to the White House. She and her children had lived in the White House 10 years earlier in 1933–1934, while separated from her first husband, stockbroker Curtis Dall.

FDR's Best Friend

The president had loyal advisors, cousins, and friends who were nearby during the war years, but his most important companion during the war years was Fala, his dog. Fala was a Scottish terrier who was born in April 1940 and was given to FDR by a woman in Connecticut, through FDR's cousin Daisy Suckley. The lively little puppy was taught several amusing tricks by Daisy before she gave him to FDR.

Murray of Fala Hill (named after a famous ancestor of FDR's; Fala for short) and FDR were inseparable during the war years. The little dog traveled virtually everywhere the president went (by car, train, and ship), and slept on a chair in the president's room. He lived at the White House beginning in November 1940, but also spent time with FDR at Warm Springs, Georgia, and at Hyde Park. Fala was even there when FDR signed

⇒ Play Charades

THE ROOSEVELTS ENJOYED playing charades with their grandchildren. Charades is a game that can be played anywhere with any number of people, and you don't need any materials. The idea is to get up in front of a few friends or family members and silently act out clues to a movie, book, song, animal, or famous person that you are thinking about. You can pick any theme you like. The game is usually good for some laughs.

YOU'LL NEED
★ 6 or more players
★ Paper
★ Pencil
★ 2 hats
★ A clear area to act out clues

Divide into two teams of three of more players each. Each team can pick a theme, such as movies, books, or animals, for the other team. Team 1 writes out different answers to the theme on small pieces of paper, folds them up, and puts them in a hat for team 2 to pick from. You should keep the answers short. One member of team 2 draws an answer from the hat to act out clues for. The other members of team 2 sit as an audience and shout out guesses. First, tell your team the category or theme (person, movie, book, etc.), but you cannot speak while acting. There are two strategies for acting out the clues. You could act out one big clue, or, if the answer is several words long, you can act out one word at a time. For example, if the movie you picked was *Star Wars*, you could act out something for "star" and then something else for "wars," or you could just think of something that would get your team to guess *Star Wars* right away.

You can hold up fingers to tell the audience how many words the clue is, and you can hold up fingers again to indicate which number word you are acting out. You can go further and indicate which syllable you are acting out. If someone guesses a word correctly, nod your head and move on to another word. Point to your ear to indicate that the clue "sounds like" if your word is too hard to act out. Once someone guesses your clue correctly, you can sit down, and it's the next team's turn. Every person on each team should get a chance to act out clues. There are no winners or losers, just a whole lot of fun.

Memories of FDR and Fala

BY ROBERT ROSENMAN,
son of Judge Samuel Rosenman, advisor to Franklin Roosevelt

"My father had been working with FDR since the time he first became governor. By 1944, he was special counsel to the president. This story took place in early September of 1944. I had just turned 13. I had returned from a summer working on a farm in a camp in Vermont. On the way back, I spent time in a house my parents rented that summer in Hyde Park. I was returning to Washington, D.C., to go back to school. I took the president's train with my father and the president and Fala. We were sitting in the parlor car in the back of the train. My father and FDR were talking. Fala was sitting on the floor sulking. He wasn't paying attention to us at all. He looked hurt. I also noticed that the president did not seem very happy. I looked at my father, and he was frantically waving at me to move off the chair where I was sitting. I moved, and all of a sudden, Fala jumped on the chair where I had been sitting. Then he was smiling and very friendly. The president smiled and was also very happy. I was sitting on the chair that was apparently reserved for Fala."

Eleanor Roosevelt, the Canadian prime minister, and Fala.

the Atlantic Charter in Quebec, Canada, in 1941. He was also with FDR when the president visited Mexico during the war.

During the presidential campaign of 1944, desperate Republicans accused FDR of leaving Fala behind on an Alaskan island and then sending a destroyer to go and get him at taxpayer expense. On September 23, 1944, FDR addressed this nasty rumor in a speech that came to be known as the "Fala speech." He said:

"*These Republican leaders have not been content with attacks on me, or my wife, or on my sons. No, not content with that, they now include my little dog, Fala. Well, of course, I don't resent attacks, and my family doesn't resent attacks, but Fala does resent them. . . . His Scotch soul was furious. He has not been the same dog since.*"

Some have called the "Fala speech" the best campaign speech FDR ever made. In the 1944 presidential campaign, it turned the tide and put the Republicans on the defensive. FDR was not just using his dog for political purposes. He truly loved Fala very much. He even preferred to feed Fala himself whenever possible.

Fala was also very popular with the press and with the American public—he even got

FDR with Fala and the granddaughter of a friend, at Hyde Park. This is one of only three existing photos of FDR in a wheelchair.

Presidential Pets

Franklin Roosevelt was not the first president to have a pet, though none was in the public eye as much as Fala. Many presidents from George Washington on have had dogs, but a few have had stranger pets. Abraham Lincoln's children had many pets in the White House including a dog, a beloved goat, and a turkey saved by presidential pardon from the Thanksgiving table. Theodore Roosevelt and his children loved animals and the family had quite a variety of pets, including a dog, cats, squirrels, a parrot, a kangaroo rat, a garter snake, and even a pony that Teddy's kids snuck into the White House elevator. President William Howard Taft had a pet cow named Pauline.

lots of fan mail of his own. A faithful companion to FDR and then, after FDR's death, to Eleanor, Fala died in his old age in 1952 and was buried next to Franklin.

Re-re-re-elect Roosevelt

As 1944 progressed, there was little discussion of whether FDR would run for president a fourth time. With the country deep into a war it now appeared to be winning, FDR did not necessarily feel comfortable turning the helm over to someone else. Still, more than ever he wished to retreat to the country and live the retired life his own father had enjoyed. In July, he told the chairman of the Democratic National Committee that he would run, but "not in the usual partisan, political sense." He went on to say that he was reluctant:

"All that is within me cries out to go back to my home on the Hudson River, to

➤ Participate in a Political Debate

FRANKLIN ROOSEVELT RAN for president and was elected four times, in 1932, 1936, 1940, and 1944. Although he would win in an electoral landslide in 1944, he did not take anything for granted. He had political enemies and knew that the Republicans would be more than happy to see him go. He knew, even in wartime, there were no guarantees that he would win. In this activity you will stage a debate, with one person playing Roosevelt and the other one of his opponents. A debate allows two candidates to each present his or her answer to a question asked by a neutral third party. Though FDR did not debate Dewey in 1944, he issued statements to counter some of Dewey's attacks.

YOU'LL NEED
- ★ 2 debators
- ★ 1 moderator
- ★ An audience
- ★ Notebook
- ★ Pen or pencil

One person will pretend to be Roosevelt, another to be his opponent, and a third to be the debate moderator. Imagine it is 1940 or 1944. The main theme of the third and fourth campaigns was the world situation. While in 1940 Willkie attacked FDR for trying to lead the United States into war, in 1944 Dewey attacked FDR for not preparing the United States enough.

FDR should make a brief speech (two to three minutes) about what his plans and goals are for his third or fourth term and what he has achieved so far. (You may want to borrow parts of speeches in this book or from the Franklin Roosevelt Library Web site www.fdrlibrary.marist.edu/firesi90.html) When FDR is done speaking, he should sit down. His opponent should stand and make a brief speech. The debate moderator should come up with three questions for each candidate. If you picked the year 1940 for your debate, one question could be "Where exactly do you stand on the United States remaining neutral?" If you picked 1944, a question could be "Why was the United States unprepared for Pearl Harbor?" The answers of the two candidates should be very different.

avoid public responsibilities, and to avoid also the publicity which in our democracy follows every step of the Nation's Chief Executive.

Such would be my choice. But we of this generation chance to live in a day and hour when our Nation has been attacked, and when its future existence and the future existence of our chosen method of government are at stake. "

FDR did not have much competition for the Democratic nomination in 1944. The Republicans were still not fans of FDR, but they knew that if the controversy about the number of terms a president should serve that had swirled around his proposed third term did not help them win in 1940, then questioning a possible fourth term would not help this time.

Another difference in 1944 was that FDR himself did not get as involved in the campaign. In fact, he might not have minded if he lost. This time around, Vice President Henry Wallace was dropped from the ticket, and the Democrats picked a Missouri senator named Harry S. Truman in his place.

A campaign song of the time was called "Let's Re-re-re-elect Roosevelt." A campaign button claimed: "We Are Going to Win This War & Win the Peace That Follows." A 1944 campaign poster featuring photos of Roosevelt and Truman said "For Lasting Peace—Security for All."

The Republicans, led by their presidential candidate New York governor Thomas Dewey, attacked FDR every chance they could. Though they could not attack him directly over the war, they could hint that he was becoming too friendly with Stalin and leaning toward the Communists. These attacks did fire up the wrath of FDR, and he fought back as the campaign wore on. In his "Fala speech" in September 1944, he said:

"The whole purpose of Republican oratory these days seems to be to switch labels. The object is to persuade the American people that the Democratic Party was responsible for the 1929 crash and the Depression, and that the Republican Party was responsible for all social progress under the New Deal.

Now, imitation may be the sincerest form of flattery—but I am afraid that in this case it is the most obvious common or garden variety of fraud. . . . Can the Old Guard pass itself off as the New Deal? I think not.

We have all seen many marvelous stunts in the circus but no performing elephant could turn a hand-spring without falling flat on his back."

Franklin and Eleanor Roosevelt with their 13 grandchildren.

FDR also attacked those Republicans who had criticized him for leading the United States to war, the same people who were now claiming they were all for the war. "What the Republican leaders are now saying in effect is this: 'Oh, just forget what we used to say, we have changed our minds now—we have been reading the public opinion polls about these things and now we know what the American people want.'"

During the final two weeks of the campaign, FDR did give speeches in New York, Philadelphia, Chicago, and Boston. At one point he told an audience he was "most anxious" to win the election. He finally ended the campaign in Worcester, Massachusetts, on November 5. When Election Day arrived on November 8, FDR defeated Dewey by a margin of 432 to 99 electoral votes, but the popular vote was fairly close at 25.6 million to 22 million.

Though it was nice to know his country still wanted him, FDR tried to prepare himself mentally for another term in office. It would be four years and two months—January 1949—before he would be free to spend his days in quiet solitude at Hyde Park and Warm Springs. At that moment in late 1944, as he sat in Hyde Park while the last of the election returns confirmed his fourth victory, his retirement seemed to him to be an eternity away.

FDR's Failing Health

The war was rapidly taking its physical toll on Franklin. In a striking parallel to what had happened to his old friend Woodrow Wilson during and after World War I, President Roosevelt was beginning to show his age. When he had first taken office 11 years earlier, he was a vibrant man of 51, paralyzed but physically strong and very active. By 1944, he was a tired 62-year-old man. No president before him had ever been in office more than eight years. The last president to serve eight full years in office had been Woodrow Wilson, who left the presidency in 1921 with his health shattered and his wife Edith serving practically as substitute president.

While Roosevelt's disability was still hidden, people could see from photos that his face looked much older than it had just a few years before. Every morning since December 1941 FDR had awoken not knowing what the day's news would bring. Would the Allies make progress? Would the Axis make advances? By 1944–1945, FDR was not a well man. He suffered from very high blood pressure and his heart was weak. He did not have anywhere near the boundless energy he had once shown. During the 1944 presidential campaign, he had experienced severe chest pains (which he insisted were due to indigestion) while talking with his son James, and had to lie down for 10 minutes. In a photo of FDR taken during his acceptance speech for the Democratic nomination, his face looked particularly gaunt and sickly. His son James would later call the 1944 campaign FDR's "death warrant."

During the winter of 1944, FDR became sick with what seemed like a very bad cold. He remained sick for a few weeks. It might have been pneumonia or bronchitis, but whatever it was, FDR suffered with it for weeks. Those who saw him in January 1945 noticed that he looked quite tired and generally gray in complexion. On Inauguration Day, January 20, he was not feeling well. To make matters worse, it was a very cold day in Washington, but FDR wore no hat or overcoat. Several of his friends and family noticed he looked sick that day. Just ahead, he had a long trip to Yalta, a resort town on the Crimean Sea, for a conference with Joseph Stalin and Winston Churchill.

FDR left Washington on January 23. He had a bad cold when he left, and over the next week it did not get better. He celebrated his 63rd birthday quietly onboard the ship. After arriving at the Mediterranean island nation of Malta, FDR transferred to a plane to make the final leg of the journey to Yalta. The conference began on February 4, and the "big three," as they were called, discussed many issues. Now that the end of the war was in sight, there was much to talk about. A photo of the "big three" shows a fragile-looking FDR wrapped in a dark cape, sitting with Churchill and Stalin.

Roosevelt, Churchill, and Stalin talked about dividing Germany after the war. Stalin wanted Germany to pay a huge amount of money to the Soviet Union to make up for all the damage that was done. The three leaders also talked about what would happen to Poland after Germany surrendered. Stalin disagreed with the other Allies about where the eastern border of Poland should be drawn. The leaders also spoke of how Poland would be governed after the war.

Another topic was the new United Nations. They debated which countries should be allowed to join the new organization, and how many votes each country would have. FDR wanted only those nations that had declared war on Germany to be eligible to join as founding members. FDR also favored one vote per country, but the insistent Soviets wound up with three votes.

During Roosevelt's time away from Washington, his daughter, Anna, who was with him at Yalta, was concerned for his health. FDR had lost weight, and was generally weak. On the voyage home at the end of February,

Winston Churchill, Franklin Roosevelt, and Joseph Stalin at Yalta, February 1945.

FDR makes his last speech to Congress, March 1945.

he could be seen sitting on the deck of the ship, staring into space.

He finally arrived in Washington on February 28, exhausted. He had worked a bit on the speech he was to give to Congress, but he had not put his usual effort into it. In his address before Congress on March 1, 1945, FDR started off with an unusual request. He asked that the members of Congress excuse him for remaining seated while giving his speech, but that he was very tired after his long trip and his leg braces were painful.

He then bent the truth when he said, "I was well the entire time. I was not ill for a second until I arrived back in Washington. There I heard all of the rumors which occurred in my absence. Yes, I returned from the trip refreshed and inspired—the Roosevelts are not, as you may suspect, averse to travel; we seem to thrive on it."

Some of those who had seen him during the first few months of 1945 said he looked like he was dying, though others felt he would shake his illness off as he had done before.

Once he had returned from his trip, FDR simply could not get back to his old self. He was mentally and physically tired. He just wanted to sleep. He went to Hyde Park for a week, but still did not feel rejuvenated. On March 17, FDR and Eleanor celebrated their 40th wedding anniversary. FDR desperately longed for Warm Springs. Between the presidential campaign, his illness, the inauguration, and the trip to Yalta, he had not had much chance for relaxation. Though Hyde Park was nice, Warm Springs was more therapeutic.

Final Days

When FDR did get down to Warm Springs at the beginning of April 1945, his doctor thought the fresh air would help him. Most of his family and friends were concerned for his health, but they had no reason to believe he would not soldier on as he had before. On this particular trip to Georgia, Eleanor remained in Washington, but two of FDR's favorite cousins and companions accompanied him. FDR took his stamp collection with him for relaxation.

FDR spent his last days peacefully at Warm Springs. It was not the ongoing war he was preoccupied with in those last days, but the postwar period and managing the peace. Stalin was being difficult about Poland and had accused Roosevelt of authorizing negotiations with the Germans behind his back. Not long before his death, FDR received a letter from Winston Churchill, who was seeking advice as to what to tell his government about British relations with the Soviets. The day of his death, Roosevelt wrote a reply to Churchill, telling his old friend that he should not make too much of the "general Soviet problem" since the Soviets seemed to be causing little crises practically every day.

The morning he died, FDR approved the design for a new stamp that was to read "Toward United Nations" with the date of April 25, 1945 (the date for the San Francisco conference). He spent some time with his own stamp collection, and finished his last speech, to be given in celebration of Thomas Jefferson's life.

A Russian portrait artist named Elizabeth Shoumatoff was busy at work painting FDR's portrait that fateful morning of April 12, 1945. At about 1 P.M., the president told the artist she would have to stop soon because it was almost time for lunch. But the lunch would go uneaten, and the portrait of FDR would go unfinished. His last words before he slumped over at 1:15 P.M. were, "I have a terrific headache." He had collapsed from a massive cerebral hemorrhage. He was quickly taken into his bedroom. His doctor tried to revive him, but the damage had been too severe. He lived for a short while longer before he died at 3:35 P.M. in his beloved "Little White House" at Warm Springs, Georgia.

Eleanor Roosevelt was notified at the White House. She sent a message to her four sons in the service that said, "Darlings: Pa slept away this afternoon. He did his job to the end as he would want you to do. Bless you. All our love, Mother."

Memories of FDR

BY MICHAEL DUKAKIS, former Massachusetts governor, Democratic presidential candidate, 1988

"You couldn't be a kid during the Depression and World War II without being very much aware of FDR. I was born in 1933, so by the end of the 1930s and during the war years, he dominated the lives of all of us. Interestingly enough, my most vivid memory of FDR is the severe aging process that seemed to take place during his last two years of life even though he was still in his early 60s. This strong, confident, and remarkably vigorous man, despite his handicap, began looking older and more and more frail in the newsreels we saw when we went to the movies, and I remember particularly how feeble he looked at Yalta in his black cape in 1945.

Of all of my FDR memories, however, the evening the word came over the radio that he had died at Warm Springs stands out in my mind. We were having dinner on our porch on an unusually warm April evening, as I recall, and suddenly the radio, which my dad insisted on having on every evening during the CBS World News Roundup at 6:00 P.M. came through with the news of his death. My parents were stunned. My brother and I had never known another president, and it was as if an era of history had ended."

7 FDR'S LEGACY

Not long after FDR's death, Eleanor Roosevelt was approached by a reporter for comment. She said quietly, "The story is over."

In fact, it was far from over. Even now, the story continues to be written. FDR's legacy continues to shape the world today. Further, Eleanor Roosevelt left behind her own mighty legacy. In the years following FDR's death, the world that FDR envisioned began to take shape, and Eleanor played a big role in carrying on her late husband's vision.

A Nation Mourns

Two hours after FDR died, Vice President Harry S. Truman arrived at the White House, where Eleanor Roosevelt broke the news to him. "Harry, the president is dead," she told him. He asked if there was anything he could do, and she replied with composure, "Is there anything we can do for you? For you are the one in trouble now."

Truman was not the only one in shock. Much of America was in a state of disbelief when they heard the news about President Roosevelt's death. After over 12 years as their leader, FDR was suddenly gone. Many people considered him a casualty of war, just as much as any soldier killed in action.

Now, less than three months after becoming vice president, Harry S. Truman was suddenly president. It would now be up to Truman to guide America to victory in Europe and then victory over Japan.

The night of FDR's death, Eleanor traveled to Warm Springs to plan the procession back to Washington, D.C., as well as the funeral. A funeral train carrying the president's body left from Warm Springs, Georgia, at 9 A.M. the next day. Along the way, thousands of people stood along the tracks to pay their respects as the train passed by. After the train's arrival at Union Station in the nation's capital, FDR's casket was drawn by six white horses toward the White House.

On Saturday, April 18, a service was held in the East Room of the White House, as FDR had requested in a sealed letter dated 1937. In that letter, FDR had made it clear that he did not want to lie in state (in which a coffin is placed on view to allow the public to pay their respects) anywhere. After the service in the White House, the casket was taken by train to Hyde Park.

On Sunday, April 19, 1945, FDR was laid to rest in the rose garden at Hyde Park as Eleanor, daughter Anna, son Elliott, and dog Fala watched. Supreme Court justices, Roosevelt cabinet members, White House staff, members of Congress, and the Canadian prime minister were also present. This was more people than FDR had directed in his instructions; he had only wanted two senators and two members of the House of Representatives. War planes circled overhead in FDR's honor. FDR's son James traveled 10,000 miles from the Pacific, but arrived too late for the funeral. His other two sons were still overseas, attending to their military duties. Eleanor asked that the grandchildren not attend; she wanted them to remember FDR alive and vibrant.

Harry S. Truman is sworn in as president, April 1945.

As he requested, a plain white marble monument (eight feet long and three feet high) was placed over the grave, with Franklin and Eleanor Roosevelt's names inscribed on it.

Now Eleanor had to move out of the White House after calling it home for over 12 years. According to FDR's wishes, his home at Hyde Park was handed over to the government soon after his death. Eleanor continued to live at the Hyde Park estate but moved permanently into Val-Kill, the nearby house that FDR had built for her in 1925 as a private retreat. Eleanor bought Val-Kill and several hundred acres of land for her own use.

One of the first things President Truman did in office was to declare a day of national mourning for Franklin D. Roosevelt. Meanwhile, messages of condolence poured in to Washington from leaders around the world, except, of course, Hitler. When Hitler and other Nazi leaders heard about FDR's death, they were delighted. Despite the bleak outlook, they took this as a positive sign.

Winston Churchill sent a message to Eleanor Roosevelt about FDR:

"I send my most profound sympathy in your grievous loss. It is also the loss of the British nation and of the cause of freedom in every land. I feel so deeply for you all. As for myself, I have lost a dear and cherished friendship which was forged in the fire of war. I trust you may find consolation in the glory of his name and the magnitude of his work."

Joseph Stalin also sent Eleanor a note, which read:

"Please accept my sincere condolence on the occasion of the death of your husband and the expression of my sincere sympathy

FDR's funeral procession in Washington, D.C., April 1945.

for your great sorrow. The Soviet people highly valued Roosevelt as a great organizer in the struggle of freedom-loving nations against the common enemy and the leader in the cause ensuring security for the whole world."

American General George C. Marshall said of the president: "We have lost a great leader. . . . No tribute from the army could be so eloquent as the hourly record of victories of the past few weeks."

On April 19, President Truman gave a speech that was broadcast to American troops around the world. He told them: "All of us have lost a great leader, a far-sighted states-man, and a real friend of democracy. You have lost a hard-hitting chief and an old friend of the services. Our hearts are heavy. However, the cause which claimed Roosevelt also claims us. He never faltered. Nor will we."

Americans across the country grieved the loss of their fallen leader. To many people in their mid- to late 20s, FDR was the only president they had ever really known during their entire lives. To many Americans, FDR was like a father figure. They trusted and admired him. Though very few people had actually met FDR, most Americans felt they knew him. He was an excellent communicator who knew how to reach the hearts and minds of the common people.

Only about a month after President Roosevelt died, the United States Mint began working on a new design for the dime, featuring FDR's portrait. On January 30, 1946, what would have been FDR's 64th birthday, the new dime was released. In part, he appeared on this coin because of his work with a charity called the March of Dimes, to prevent birth defects.

A memorial for FDR in the nation's capital was planned as early as 1955, but years of debate over various proposals for the design delayed the process. The FDR Memorial was finally dedicated in Washington, D.C., in 1997. Though FDR had hidden the severity of his disability from the public, a 10-foot-high statue of FDR in a wheelchair graces the memorial.

"FDR TRANSFORMED MY LIFE, THE LIVES OF THOSE AROUND ME, AND THE LIFE OF OUR NATION."

—Jimmy Carter, president of the United States, 1977–1981

Aftermath of FDR's Presidency

The war in Europe progressed quickly after FDR's death. By the end of April, the American army met up with the Soviet army in Germany, and Hitler committed suicide before the Allies could get to him. On May 2, the Germans in Italy gave up, and on May 8, VE-day (Victory in Europe), Germany surrendered to the Allies unconditionally.

Unfortunately, the war in the Pacific was not quite over. Fierce fighting continued through May, June, and July. In early August 1945, President Truman ordered that the newly developed atomic bomb be dropped on Japan. FDR had insisted that there were "many roads to Tokyo," but by the summer of 1945, options seemed more limited. To Truman, it seemed the only way to avoid months more of fighting and thousands more American casualties was to use the newly developed technology.

The first atomic bomb was dropped on the city of Hiroshima, and then, on August 9, a second bomb was dropped on the city of Nagasaki. More than 120,000 Japanese were killed. On August 15, 1945, the Japanese surrendered. The war that FDR had led America through almost to the end was finally over.

FDR REVIEWED EVERY stamp that was issued while he was president. He even helped design some stamps. After his death, he was honored by a series of four stamps in 1945–1946 and was also honored on a stamp issued during the 1960s. In this activity you will come up with an idea for a new stamp.

YOU'LL NEED
★ Pen and paper (or computer)
★ Stamp price guide (such as *The Official Blackbook Price Guide of United States Postage Stamps*)
★ Stamped envelope

How are new stamps created? Nearly every stamp issued by the United States Postal Service originated with an idea submitted by an ordinary American citizen. The 15-person Citizens' Stamp Advisory Committee (CSAC) considers all ideas, working with the Postal Service to sort through the 50,000 notes it receives every year. All suggestions are considered; the committee is looking for subjects that are "both interesting and educational."

Is there an FDR-related topic that might be relevant to submit? Get or borrow a stamp price guide, and review some of the stamp subjects of the last 20 years. Is there a person, place, thing, or event that is missing and that should be honored with a stamp? Keep in mind that no living person can be featured on U.S. postage.

Submit your idea to the following address. If you have an idea for a timely stamp (commemorating an anniversary of a birth, death, or event), you need to submit the idea at least three years before the event. You don't need to draw a picture, just write your idea in a letter.

Citizens' Stamp Advisory Committee
Stamp Development
US Postal Service
1735 North Lynn Street, Room 5013
Arlington, VA 22209-6432

German tank surrenders to the Allies in May 1945.

As the 1950s and 1960s progressed, the Soviets tried to spread their communist influence to Asia. Soviet leader Nikita Khrushchev's declaration to the United States that "we will bury you" was a far cry from Stalin's commitment to help the United States. It was the Cold War, and it would last for over 40 years. The role of the new United Nations was to be extremely important in the complicated postwar world. FDR was right about something else—without the United States, the United Nations would not have succeeded.

Eleanor in the Spotlight

Eleanor Roosevelt did not settle into the life of retirement that she surely deserved. Though many years before, she would have longed for the day when she was out of the public spotlight, Eleanor continued to be a public figure after Franklin's death. People still associated Eleanor with her late husband, but she continued to make her own name in history. In fact, more than any other first lady, Eleanor Roosevelt gained fame and respect in the years after she left the White House.

Though she could have easily run for Congress or perhaps an even higher office, Eleanor did not wish to run for elected office. An opportunity soon came up that she could not resist. President Truman called her in Decem-

Over the next year, battle-weary soldiers began to return home.

As FDR had imagined, the peace that followed the war was to be complicated. The Soviets occupied part of Germany, and the city of Berlin was split into two zones (eventually the Berlin Wall was erected). The Soviets also occupied several countries in Eastern Europe. Thus began a strange new war, mostly a war of nerves (rather than blood) at the beginning.

ber 1945. He wanted to name her as one of the five U.S. delegates to the United Nations (UN) and have her attend the first session in London.

She soon became involved in the United Nations Commission for Human Rights, where she was selected as the chairperson. Eleanor Roosevelt worked hard to write a Universal Declaration of Human Rights. This was no easy task, because she had to coordinate, debate, and negotiate with delegates from more than 50 other nations over the wording of the document. It seemed a fitting role for her, considering that some of the document addressed the four freedoms that FDR had first mentioned in 1941.

"I COULD NOT AT ANY AGE BE CONTENT TO TAKE MY PLACE IN A CORNER BY THE FIRESIDE AND SIMPLY LOOK ON."

—Eleanor Roosevelt

Memories of Eleanor Roosevelt

BY JEANE KIRKPATRICK,
U.S. ambassador to the United Nations, 1981–1985

"Eleanor Roosevelt worked hard on the U.N. Human Rights Commission. Her sons told me that they thought of her when they saw me working late on a Human Rights task or when they heard a good debate on human rights. She was energetic, even indefatigable, and truly untiring in her work on human rights. Her sons were proud of the work their mother did on this task, and I think we were all proud of her work."

For example, there was tension with the Soviet delegates over a phrase that read: "Everyone has the right to freedom of movement and residence within the borders of each state. Everyone has the right to leave any country, including his own, and return to his country." The Soviets wanted to change that to "Everyone has the right to leave any country, including his own, and to return to his country according to the laws of his country." Through much negotiation and perseverance, Eleanor Roosevelt was able to help create a document that could be embraced by all UN countries.

In December 1948, Eleanor Roosevelt told the UN General Assembly: "We stand today at the threshold of a great event both in the life of the United Nations and in the life of mankind. This declaration may well become the international Magna Carta for all men everywhere." Some of the provisions of the final document were:

> Article 12: *No one shall be subjected to arbitrary interference with his privacy, family, home or correspondence, nor to attacks upon his honour and reputation. Everyone has the right to the protection of the law against such interference or attacks.*

> Article 18: *Everyone has the right to freedom of thought, conscience and religion; this right includes freedom to change his religion or belief, and freedom, either alone or in community with others and in public or private, to manifest his religion or belief in teaching, practice, worship and observance.*

> Article 19: *Everyone has the right to freedom of opinion and expression; this*

Eleanor Roosevelt with FDR Jr. and FDR III in 1962.

right includes freedom to hold opinions without interference and to seek, receive and impart information and ideas through any media and regardless of frontiers.

The General Assembly voted in favor of the document 48–0.

That document was just one of Eleanor's many triumphs in her later years. She continued to write her newspaper column, "My Day," until shortly before her death. She also had her own television show. She remained politically active, and in 1956 and 1960 supported Democrat Adlai Stevenson's bid for the presidency. When Eleanor Roosevelt died in 1962 at the age of 78, the public mourned her death just as intensely as it had FDR's 17 years earlier.

FDR's Children

The Roosevelt children led rich and complex lives. All of them were married more than once, and all were in the public spotlight over the course of their lives. As the Roosevelt "chicks" found out, it was both a blessing and a curse to be the children of Franklin and Eleanor Roosevelt.

Anna Roosevelt was a writer and the editor of a major Seattle newspaper. She was married

Memories of Eleanor Roosevelt

BY GERALDINE FERRARO, congresswoman and Democratic candidate for vice president, 1984

"I met Eleanor Roosevelt once in 1961, when I was a newly married young lawyer. She was someone I had admired as a child since my family truly adored the president. I remember thinking when I saw her that she seemed to be 10 feet tall, but I guess it was just her presence that made her so imposing.

What was interesting was that she truly was a woman who was ahead of her time both as first lady, redefining that job, and later as a leader in her own right. In 1984 I was thrilled that we could schedule the one vice presidential debate I would participate in to take place on her 100th birthday because, though she had never run for office, I considered her a role model. And in 1993, when President Clinton nominated me as the U.S. ambassador to the United Nations Human Rights Commission, I was honored to be able to serve in a body that she had created almost 50 years before. She was a woman who achieved her position in American history because of the man she married. But she was a woman who achieved her place in the hearts of Americans because of the things she did."

three times and was the first of the Roosevelt children to die, in 1975.

James Roosevelt worked as an insurance broker after graduating from Harvard in 1930. He later served as a special secretary to his father in 1937–1938. After the war, he was a businessman and politician. He ran unsuccessfully for governor of California in 1950. He served in Congress from 1955 to 1965. He died in 1991.

Elliott Roosevelt lived at Hyde Park for seven years after his father's death. He served as mayor of Miami Beach, Florida, from 1965 to 1969. He wrote several nonfiction and fiction books, including mystery novels. He was married five times and died in 1990.

Franklin D. Roosevelt Jr. was a lawyer and the vice president of President Truman's committee on civil rights, and also a congressman (1949–1955). He tried unsuccessfully to obtain the Democratic nomination for governor of New York in 1954. President Kennedy appointed him undersecretary of commerce, and President Johnson appointed him chairman of the Equal Employment Opportunity Commission. He died in 1988.

John Roosevelt, the youngest child, became a Republican in 1952 and supported Dwight D. Eisenhower's bid for the presidency. He was active in several organizations, including the Boy Scouts (like his father). He filled out his days as a businessman, never becoming a politician. He died in 1981.

The first of the many Roosevelt grandchildren (Anna's daughter) was born in 1927, and the last (FDR Jr.'s son) in 1977. The descendants of Franklin Delano Roosevelt are spread across the country, in all walks of life.

In the years following Franklin Roosevelt's death, nearly everyone who had been in his administration wrote books about him. Everyone had a story to tell about how FDR had responded to the Depression, his friendship with Churchill, or how he had dealt with Stalin. From the late 1940s and even through the 1960s, many historians were uncertain of FDR's place in history. Was he a fearless leader? Was he an aristocratic tyrant? His biggest fans put him on a pedestal as a truly great president in a time of great crisis. His critics accused him of faulty New Deal policies that did not really lead the United States out of the Depression. They said he created "big government" that was too involved in people's lives. They said he was unsteady on his foreign policy, promising to keep America out of the war but secretly trying to get the United States involved. They accused him of giving in to Stalin's demands.

Time has given us some perspective. Many historians today believe that FDR was one of the greatest presidents of the 20th century, and among the top three presidents who ever lived. His legacy of social security has provided millions of retired Americans with money to help them live out their years. His WPA programs have left a rich legacy of public works, have helped rejuvenate the environment, have preserved songs and folklore of a bygone era, and have given us large-scale artworks all across the country. His economic programs ensure that our money is safe in the bank (insured by the federal government up to $100,000).

FDR was a president of the people. He led them through the Depression and he led them through World War II. Overall, his approach to the presidency can best be summed up in his own words, from a fireside chat he gave in 1938:

"I try always to remember that their [Americans'] deepest problems are human. I constantly talk with those who come to tell me their own points of view—with those who manage the great industries and financial institutions of the country—with those who represent the farmer and the worker—and often, very often with average citizens without high position who come to this house. And constantly I seek to look beyond the doors of the White House, beyond the officialdom of the National Capital, into the hopes and fears of men and women in their homes. I have travelled the country over many times. My friends, my enemies, my daily mail bring to me reports of what you are thinking and hoping. I want to be sure that neither battles nor burdens of office shall ever blind me to an intimate knowledge of the way the American people want to live and the simple purposes for which they put me here."

★ ★ ★ ★ ★ ★

PLACES TO VISIT

Eleanor Roosevelt National Historic Site
Located on Route 9G in the town of Hyde
   Park, New York.
(800) 337-8474
www.nps.gov/elro
The site of Val-Kill, the cottage in Hyde Park that served first as Eleanor's retreat and later her home after FDR's death.

The Franklin and Eleanor Roosevelt Institute (online only)
www.feri.org
This Web site is the home for an organization dedicated to preserving the legacy of the 32nd president. There are several good resources on this site, including biographies and background information on FDR, the text of some speeches, and links to other sites.

Franklin D. Roosevelt American Heritage Center Museum
Second floor of Union Station
2 Washington Square
Worcester, Massachusetts
(508) 770-1515
www.fdrheritage.org
This museum contains photos and mementos of FDR's life. The Web site also has some background information on FDR and Eleanor Roosevelt.

Franklin D. Roosevelt Presidential Library and Museum
4079 Albany Post Road
Hyde Park, New York
(800) FDR-VISIT or (845) 486-7770
www.fdrlibrary.marist.edu

The FDR Library and Museum showcase FDR's home and his presidential library. The library is an excellent place for research on FDR. The Web site also contains thousands of photos and documents relating to FDR, as well as biographies of FDR, Eleanor Roosevelt, and other key people in FDR's life.

Franklin Delano Roosevelt Memorial
Located along the Cherry Tree Walk on the Western edge of the Tidal Basin near the National Mall, Washington, D.C.
(202) 426-6841
www.nps.gov/fdrm
This recently built memorial to FDR depicts him in a wheelchair. It also depicts his dog, Fala. The Web site has some facts about the memorial and its displays.

Roosevelt Campobello International Park
Located two miles from the International Bridge on Campobello Island, New Brunswick, Canada, off the coast of Maine.
(506) 752-2922
www.nps.gov/roca/index.htm
This park is a joint memorial to FDR run by Canada and the United States. Located within are 2,800 acres of natural areas, as well as the Roosevelt cottage, the site of the Roosevelt's summer home since 1886.

Roosevelt's Little White House Historic Site
401 Little White House Road
Warm Springs, Georgia
(706) 655-5870
www.fdr-littlewhitehouse.org
FDR's Warm Springs cottage has been preserved, much as it appeared the day he died in 1945. The Web site has a brochure and other information about the museum.

Roosevelt Railroad Museum
3030 Teamon Road
Griffin, Spalding County, Georgia
(770) 228-7519
www.rooseveltrailroad.com
During his lifetime, President Roosevelt made more than 50 trips by railroad while traveling between Washington, D.C., and Warm Springs, Georgia. This museum is dedicated to preserving the legacy of FDR's extensive rail travel in Georgia.

BIBLIOGRAPHY

(Books noted by ★ are suitable for kids ages nine and older)

★ Axelrod, Alan. *Nothing to Fear: Lessons in Leadership from FDR*. New York: Portfolio, 2003.

Barnes, Harry Elmer, ed. *Perpetual War for Perpetual Peace*. Idaho: The Caxton Printers, Ltd., 1953.

Burns, James MacGregor. *Roosevelt: The Lion and the Fox*. New York: Harcourt, Brace & World, Inc., 1956.

Cook, Blanche Wiesen. *Eleanor Roosevelt, Volume 2, 1933–1938*. New York: Viking, 1999.

Eisenhower, Dwight D. *Crusade in Europe*. Garden City, New York: Doubleday & Company, Inc., 1948.

Ferrell, Robert H. *The Dying President: Franklin D. Roosevelt 1944–1945*. Columbia, Missouri: University of Missouri Press, 1998.

Freidel, Frank. *Franklin D. Roosevelt: The Apprenticeship*. Boston: Little, Brown and Company, 1952.

Gallagher, Hugh Gregory. *FDR's Splendid Deception*. New York: Dodd, Mead & Company, 1985.

★ Graves, Charles P. *Eleanor Roosevelt*. New York: Dell Publishing Co, Inc., 1966.

Ickes, Harold L. *The Secret Diary of Harold L. Ickes: The First Thousand Days, 1933–1936*. New York: Simon and Schuster, 1953.

Lash, Joseph P. *Eleanor and Franklin*. New York: W.W. Norton & Company, Inc., 1971.

Lash, Joseph P. *Eleanor: The Years Alone*. New York: W.W. Norton & Company, Inc., 1972.

Lindley, Ernest K. *Franklin D. Roosevelt: A Career in Progressive Democracy*. New York: Blue Ribbon Books, Inc., 1934.

★ Perkins, Frances. *The Roosevelt I Knew*. New York: The Viking Press, 1946.

Persico, Joseph E. *Roosevelt's Secret War: FDR and World War II Espionage*. New York: Random House Trade Paperbacks, 2002.

★ Pottker, Jan. *Sara and Eleanor*. New York: St. Martin's Griffin, 2004.

Rollins, Alfred B. Jr. *Roosevelt and Howe*. New York: Alfred A. Knopf, 1962.

★ Roosevelt, David B. *Grandmere: A Personal History of Eleanor Roosevelt*. New York: Warner Books, 2002.

★ Roosevelt, Eleanor. *This Is My Story*. New York: Harper & Brothers, 1937.

★ Roosevelt, Eleanor. *My Day: The Best of Eleanor Roosevelt's Acclaimed Newspaper Columns, 1936–1962*. New York: MJF Books, 2001.

★ Roosevelt, Elliott, ed. *The Roosevelt Letters, Volumes One, Two, and Three*. London: George G. Harrap & Co. Ltd. 1950–52.

Roosevelt, James and Sidney Shalett. *Affectionately, F.D.R.: A Son's Story of a Lonely Man*. New York: Harcourt, Brace and Com pany, 1959.

★ Roosevelt, Sara Delano. *My Boy Franklin*. New York: Ray Long & Richard R. Smith, Inc., 1933.

Sherwood, Robert E. *Roosevelt and Hopkins: An Intimate History*. New York: Harper & Brothers, 1948.

Welles, Sumner. *The Time for Decision*. New York: Harper & Brothers, 1944.

INDEX

★ ★ ★ ★ ★ ★

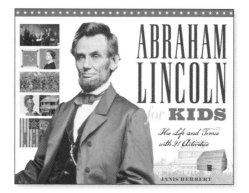